# Around the World
## in a
# Napier

# AROUND THE WORLD
## IN A
# NAPIER
## THE STORY OF
## TWO MOTORING PIONEERS

ANDREW M. JEPSON

FOREWORD BY GEOFF MCGARRY
PRESIDENT OF THE NAPIER POWER HERITAGE TRUST

The
History
Press

*For my mother*
*who remembered much*
*and discovered more*

*and*

*For Bob*
*who filled in*
*the blanks*

*Cover illustrations. Front:* The Glidden party in Ceylon. (Author's collection) *Back, top left:* Burmese temple (author's collection); *top right:* Maoris gather by the car in their village near Rotorua (author's collection); *bottom right:* a Chinese wheelbarrow. (Author's collection)

First published 2013

The History Press
The Mill, Brimscombe Port
Stroud, Gloucestershire, GL5 2QG
www.thehistorypress.co.uk

© Andrew M. Jepson, 2013

The right of Andrew M. Jepson to be identified as the Author
of this work has been asserted in accordance with the
Copyright, Designs and Patents Act 1988.

British Library Cataloguing in Publication Data.
A catalogue record for this book is available from the British Library.

ISBN 978 0 7524 9773 0
Typesetting and origination by The History Press
Printed in Great Britain

# CONTENTS

# LIST OF MAPS

# Foreword

It is an honour and a great pleasure to be writing this introduction to Andrew Jepson's fascinating book describing the exploits of his grandfather, Charles Thomas, as the travelling mechanic to Charles Glidden on his world tours in a Napier motor car.

From our present advantage of reliable, easily purchased motor cars, it is amazing to look back at a story from the dawn of motoring. Cars then were the preserve of the moneyed few, costing well beyond the means of the great majority. Charles Glidden was in the fortunate position of making a substantial sum of money – a millionaire of his day – at a comparatively young age. He was clearly fascinated by new technology and, when he became interested in the motor car, by the challenge of driving the car to parts of the world where proper roads were often non-existent and the car itself an object of novelty and suspicion.

The firm of D. Napier & Son traces its roots back to the early nineteenth century, with a reputation for fine precision-engineering that has been its hallmark through its 200-year history to the present day. Shortly after grandson Montague Napier took over control of the company in 1895, he turned his attention to motor cars. It was a happy coincidence that close friend and fellow club cyclist Selwyn Francis Edge asked Montague Napier to make improvements to his Panhard et Levassor car and from this initial foray, D. Napier & Son became a successful producer of motor cars. Applying their precision-engineering expertise allowed them to refine and produce cars of exceptional quality equal to the continental competition.

Success of one of the earliest of these cars in the Round-Britain Thousand-Mile Trial of 1900 was followed by the first international victory by a British car in the 1902 Gordon Bennett race. It is perhaps from publicity such as this that Charles Glidden came to select a Napier car for his travels round the world. Napier went on to set records at Brooklands and provided the famous Lion engine which powered record breakers on land, sea and in the air, as well as a succession of other famous engines through to the 1960s. I was privileged to work for Napier in the post-war period and can attest to their pursuit of engineering excellence in all that they achieved, and still achieve today as manufacturers of turbochargers.

The Napier Power Heritage Trust was established in 1993, with the dedicated aim of researching and preserving Napier engineering history for the advancement of heritage and education in the development of engines and the importance of D. Napier & Son's contribution to that history. With over 200 members, it is a registered charity that produces a quarterly journal, *Napier Heritage News*, and has gathered together a substantial historical archive and assisted in the publication of a number of books on Napier engines. Further details, including membership or requests for information, can be found at: www.napierheritage.org.uk.

I am delighted that, with this latest publication, an important historical account of early motoring and a testament to Napier engineering will reach a wider audience.

*Geoff McGarry*
*President, Napier Power Heritage Trust*

# INTRODUCTION

During the 1920s my mother, at that time a teenager living with her parents, found an old biscuit tin tucked away at the back of a cupboard. It contained hundreds of photographs taken in many far-flung corners of the world. They showed her father, Charles Thomas, who, as a young man, had been employed as chauffeur-mechanic by the American millionaire Charles Jasper Glidden. In the first decade of the twentieth century Glidden, assisted by Charles Thomas, drove his Napier car around the world not once but twice.

My mother pasted the photographs into a series of albums and persuaded her reluctant father to write captions under some of them. There the matter rested.

The albums survived the Great Depression, the Second World War and many house moves until, in retirement, my mother determined to piece together the entire story. The task took her the best part of two decades, during which she corresponded with universities, city archives and local history societies in Canada, New Zealand, New England, Sweden and France.

Her researches were greatly assisted by a relative whose internet skills enabled him to acquire copies of newspapers and motoring magazines dating from the 1900s which contained reports of Glidden's journeys. The main sources of information for this were the *Boston Globe* and *Sunday Globe*, which published Glidden's letters, and *The Autocar* magazine.

Before her death, my mother succeeded in gathering all the information needed to tell the story of her father's travels. This mass of documents then passed to me, together with what was, by now, a very battered set of albums. Many of the photographs had faded and despite, or perhaps because of, my mother's teenage enthusiasm, not all were in the correct order. Going through them I found images of Fiji alongside those of the north-west frontier of India and many other similar discrepancies.

The captions my grandfather had written more than a decade after the event were not always accurate and a large number of the photographs remained unlabelled. Peering out of them were nameless individuals wearing exotic costume, the inhabitants of places unknown.

Computer technology has enhanced faded images revealing, for the first time in many years, clues, such as road signs, allowing some locations to be identified. Through careful reading of the documents many of the faces do now have names and their stories can be told. From among the many hundreds of photographs contained in the albums I have chosen the most interesting and significant. They provide an opportunity to look back on an era, now gone from living memory, when the motor car was nothing but a rich man's toy and, for good or ill, the great European empires were at their height.

My mother was not given time to form the results of her research into a single narrative. This volume is my attempt to complete her work.

*Andrew Jepson*
*July 2013*

# 1

# CHARLES THOMAS

Charles Thomas was born on 11 June 1881, the son of Frederick Thomas of Rottingdean in Sussex, a hotelier and horse bus proprietor.

The England of Victorian and Edwardian times was dominated by class distinction and Charles grew up seeing how his father's hotel provided deferential service for wealthy people. Those who knew him in later life described him as being very kind, mild and conscientious.

A frequent guest at the hotel was the entrepreneur Selwyn Edge, who noticed the young boy's interest in the early motor vehicles whose owners also stayed at the hotel. Edge recommended Charles to his friend and business associate

Charles Thomas. (Author's collection)

Montague Napier and, on 13 January 1895, Charles Thomas took up the offer of an engineering apprenticeship with the Napier Company.

On completing his apprenticeship, Charles went to work for Edge at the Motor Power Company. Edge had negotiated the sole concession to sell Napier cars, an arrangement that lasted for almost a decade and a half, during which Napier gained the premier position in motoring and motor racing.

In 1901 Edge sold a Napier to the maharajah of Balrampur and Charles was entrusted with the task of delivering the car to India. He travelled with it to Bombay, saw it safely landed on the dockside and drove it to Balrampur, near the frontier with Nepal, a journey of more than 700 miles over tracks where it must have been among the first, perhaps the very first, powered vehicle ever seen.

Teaching the maharajah to drive was not without incident. The royal bodyguard had to stand in the back of the Napier but its members were all terrified because of their elderly master's tendency to fall asleep at the wheel. At the end of a drive they would be entirely smothered in dust. Charles lived with the maharajah for a year, teaching not only him but many of his court to drive.

Meanwhile, on the other side of the world, events were taking place that would have a profound effect upon the course of Charles Thomas's life. Those events were initiated by Charles J. Glidden.

# 2

# CHARLES J. GLIDDEN

Charles Jasper Glidden was born in Lowell, Massachusetts, on 29 August 1857, the son of a foundry worker. At the age of 15, after completing his education in the municipal schools, Glidden began his first job, as a messenger for the Northern Telegraph Company on Central Street. He became a skilled telegrapher and acquired a good technical knowledge of the system. A year later he gained the position of night manager for the Franklin Telegraph Company in Springfield, Massachusetts. Such was his business ability that within a month he was promoted to manager at the company's office in Manchester, New Hampshire, where he served from 1873 to 1877. During this period he also acted as local correspondent for the *Boston Globe*, a connection from which he was to benefit when, as a

Charles J. Glidden. (Author's collection)

famous pioneer motorist, that newspaper published his letters describing journeys in many different lands.

While in Manchester, Glidden connected clients to the telegraph office by wire, thus avoiding the need to employ messengers. In 1876 he met Alexander Graham Bell, inventor of the telephone, and they arranged to test whether speech could be transmitted over the telegraph lines. The tests, carried out in the presence of the state governor and the city's mayor, demonstrated that the telephone would function as a practical means of communication.

Resigning from his position with Franklin Telegraph, Glidden now became increasingly involved with the development of the telephone and supervised the installation of private telephone lines in Massachusetts and New Hampshire. He originated the idea of the telephone exchange and suggested that the Bell Company build such a system. The company agreed, on condition that he found fifty clients willing to pay a subscription of $1.50 a month. He accomplished this task, acquiring the necessary number of clients with ease. The owners of Lowell's many cotton mills, realising how their businesses would benefit, were particularly eager to subscribe.

On 19 April 1878 his invention, the first telephone exchange in the world, was opened at 36 Central Street, Lowell, with the lines let into the building through an open skylight.

On 10 July he married Lucy Emma Clegworth of New Hampshire and on 29 August celebrated his twenty-first birthday.

The following year he built the world's first long-distance telephone line from Lowell to Boston, surveying the route in person and arranging the necessary rights of way. Then, together with a group of associates, he formed a business syndicate which bought the Lowell Telephone Exchange from the Bell Company. The syndicate organised telephone exchanges throughout New England. Glidden served as treasurer of several telephone companies and was secretary of New England Telephone. The syndicate flourished and by 1883 it had interests in telephone and telegraph companies in Minnesota, Arkansas, South Dakota, Texas and Ohio. In June of that year they formed the Erie Telephone and Telegraph Company. By 1897 Glidden's original fifty subscribers had increased to 46,000.

New England society of the time expected successful businessmen to enter into the wider civic and religious life of their communities. For Glidden, raised as a Methodist, it was a natural thing for him to do, but, as a self-made man, he probably realised it would also help maintain and enhance the level of social standing to which he had risen. Thus prompted, he became a trustee and treasurer of St Paul's Methodist Episcopal Church, taking a keen interest in its benevolent work.

As he helped develop one new technology his attention was caught by another, the automobile. In 1898 he acquired three electric cars; one he kept in his home town of Lowell, another in Boston and the third in New York. No doubt they helped him go about both his business and social life but they were limited to a range of 15 miles. He solved the problem of making longer journeys by having spare batteries kept at convenient places in all three cities.

In January 1901 Glidden's group sold its interests in the Erie Telephone and Telegraph Company to a banking syndicate. He resigned as company president but continued as a director. At the age of 43 he retired a very wealthy man.

Having made his millions he determined to spend some of them on the purchase of a motor car, not merely as an urban runabout but to travel the world. Motor transport would, he believed, have an impact upon society as great as, or greater than, the telephone. He therefore wanted to foster American interest in this new industry and encourage the necessary improvement of the nation's roads.

As a true Yankee patriot Glidden might have been expected to buy an American vehicle; instead he chose a British model. His attention may have been caught by news of a 1,000-mile trial held in 1900, in which a car manufactured by the firm of D. Napier & Son did particularly well.

# 3

# D. NAPIER & SON – MAKER OF THE GLIDDEN CARS

The company of D. Napier & Son traces its roots back to 1808, when David Napier came from Scotland to establish an engineering business in London, making printing presses. He was joined in 1845 by his son and apprentice James, and the company established a new works in Vine Street, Lambeth, producing hydraulic hoists for the railways, boring and other machines for the Woolwich Arsenal, and precision balances for the Royal Mint.

James was a prolific inventor and patentee, introducing machines to perforate postage stamps as well as ever-more sophisticated printing presses, coin-making and weighing machines. However, technological change in the second half of the nineteenth century was very rapid and the Lambeth works failed to keep pace. By the time of James's death in 1896 his business had declined.

James's youngest son, Montague Stanley Napier, rose to the challenge: at the age of 25 he took over the Vine Street works, reviving the company's coin-weighing and other precision-engineering activities. In character he was gentlemanly but taciturn, suitable attributes for an engineer, less so for a salesman. To capitalise on the new world of the motor car he therefore needed the aid of a publicist and sportsman just as, a few years later, Charles Rolls helped promote Henry Royce.

Selwyn Francis Edge was born in Australia but moved to Upper Norwood, England, with his parents and was educated at Belvedere House College. As a teenager he discovered competitive cycling, specialising in 100-mile contests on the Great North and London to Brighton roads, in the course of which he demonstrated not only his physical endurance but also great mental persistence and determination.

Edge had his first experience of a motor car on the streets of Paris in 1895. The car was a 6hp Panhard et Levassor owned by fellow champion cyclist Fernand

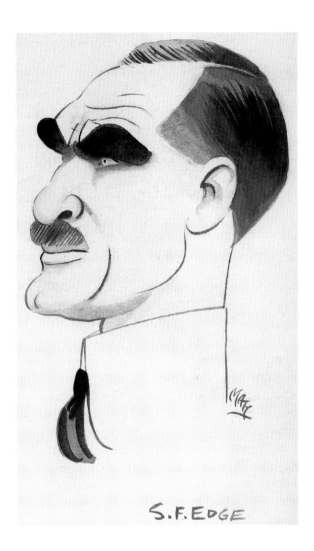

Caricature of S.F. Edge. (Courtesy of D.R. Grossmark, NPHT Registrar)

S.F. EDGE

Charron. In his autobiography, *My Motoring Reminiscences*, he wrote, 'I returned to England next day, with the fixed determination that I would leave no stone unturned to advance the cause of the automobile.' In 1897, drawing on his cycling experience, Edge started touring and racing de Dion-Bouton and Leon Bollée tricycles, with some success. With the backing of Harvey Du Cros, who had purchased the patents for the Dunlop pneumatic tyre, Edge became manager of the Dunlop Tyre Company.

In 1899 Edge purchased a Panhard et Levassor racing car from Henry Lawson. The car had already taken part in the 1896 Paris-Marseilles race and needed to be updated. Walter Munn, a friend and fellow member of the Bath Road Cycling Club, suggested Montague Napier as the ideal person to undertake the modifications. These included converting it from tiller to wheel steering, fitting a radiator and, in due course, a new engine of Napier's own design. Edge wrote in his autobiography, 'After giving this engine a thorough trial and comparing this car with when I first bought it, I was convinced that in Napier I had had the good fortune to alight on a motor engineer of outstanding ability.'

In the autumn of 1899 an agreement was drawn up granting S.F. Edge the sole right to sell Napier cars through the Motor Power Company which, with backing from Du Cros, he had formed in premises at 14 Regent Street, London.

Napier would initially build three two-cylinder cars and three four-cylinder cars. The Motor Power Company also had agencies for Clement and Gladiator cars.

In April 1900 Edge entered a two-cylinder Napier in a 1,000-mile trial. It came first in its class and won a silver-gilt medal for the second-best performance in the whole trial (Charles Rolls was first, driving a Panhard). This began a series of successful exploits in which S.F. Edge drove Napier cars competitively, proving their speed and durability. Of particular note was his victory in the 1902 Gordon Bennett Trophy race – the first time a British-built car won an international event.

Perhaps attracted by Edge's success, Charles J. Glidden chose one of the early four-cylinder Napier cars for his 1901 tour of Britain and France and was so impressed that he purchased two more; the second he used in 1902 for a tour of central and southern Europe; the third, even more powerful car, he used in 1903 to cross the Arctic Circle. This third car proved so reliable that Glidden continued to use it until 1908, during which time he twice drove around the world.

Ever the publicist, Edge made use of these exploits in his sales catalogues and advertisements, printing Glidden's testimonials alongside those of other satisfied customers.

# 4

# First Encounter

Charles Thomas was still in India when, on 9 July 1901, Glidden took delivery of his first Napier. He had ordered the car by cable from Boston with instructions that it be brought to London's Victoria Hotel, in Northumberland Avenue, at eight o'clock on the morning of the 9th. When it arrived, he was there to take delivery and, having no experience of petrol-powered vehicles, asked Napier's representative to explain the purpose of the various controls, after which he took the driver's seat and made his first day's run of 120 miles, reaching Stratford-upon-Avon that evening.

Glidden's first Napier. (Courtesy of Clive Boothman of the NPHT / *The Autocar*)

The car, a type H70 with a chassis price of £1,200, was powered by a four-cylinder, 4942cc engine, rated at 16hp. Each cylinder had a bore of 4 inches and a piston stroke of 6 inches with auto inlet valves and side exhaust. The wheelbase was 7ft 8in with a track width of 4ft 1½in. Front suspension was half elliptic and the rear suspension full elliptic. A chain drive was used in the final stage of transmission. The car's coachwork and upholstery were supplied by the Northampton firm Mulliners.

In this car Glidden covered large parts of England, driving as far north as Sheffield and Halifax without mishap, after which he returned to Folkestone and crossed to Boulogne. The next few days were spent motoring across Normandy, through Dieppe and Rouen, before entering Paris. The car broke a front spring by running over a high curb in the village of St Ledger but Glidden was able to effect a temporary repair and continue on to Chartres, where a new spring was obtained and fitted.

On 1 August Glidden left Chartres for Tours and Angers, where he stayed for the weekend. He intended to drive on to Nantes but soon after starting an exhaust valve lifted off the cam-shaft, resulting in complete loss of power. Local repair was impossible; the engine needed to be completely disassembled and the necessary spare parts could only come from London. Glidden contacted Edge by telegraph and three days later a Napier engineer arrived to carry out the work.

Glidden's 1902 Napier. (Author's collection)

Well pleased with his first 2,000-mile tour, Glidden placed an order with the Motor Power Company for a second Napier and returned to America, already formulating plans for another tour the following year. Learning of Glidden's intentions, the US State Department asked him to report on the condition of road networks wherever he travelled.

In July 1902, within hours of arriving in London, Glidden commenced his second tour, having travelled from Boston aboard the liner *Lucania*. The new car was the 16hp Napier that had won the concourse d'elegance at the Crystal Palace Show in February that year. He was accompanied by his wife and two close friends, Mr and Mrs Dudley E. Waters of Grand Rapids, Michigan.

At this time, motor companies often provided their wealthiest clients with a trained engineer to maintain the vehicle and carry out repairs at the roadside. After the delays experienced in France the previous year, Glidden would have understood that, if his plans were to be realised, such an arrangement was necessary. Selwyn Edge, sensing potential for much valuable marketing publicity, offered Glidden the services of his employee, Charles Thomas, who was initially reluctant to take on the role. He had already spent a year away in India and wished to resume his family and social life at home. However, Edge was not to be denied; astute and forceful, he wrote a letter presenting the job as a unique opportunity for advancement. Edge may also have used the fact that Charles Thomas was, like Glidden and himself, a Freemason. Raised in an age of deference, and already obligated to Edge for his apprenticeship with Napier, Charles accepted.

It is clear from contemporary reports in *The Autocar* that the route was meticulously planned to take in the fashionable European resorts. Starting at the Channel port of Dieppe, they headed south-east to Metz and along the Saar and Moselle valleys, then up the Rhine to Koblenz and Heidelberg, through the Black Forest and Baden-Baden to Neuhausen and the Rhine Falls, thence to Konstanz on the Bodensee and over the Arlberg Pass to Innsbruck. They crossed Austria to the Brenner Pass and into Italy at Vitipeno, from there going on to visit Venice, Verona and the Italian lakes. Selwyn Edge received a postcard from Brescia dated 7 August 1902 in which Glidden stated they had driven 1,666 miles in seventeen days without any misadventure. Next they crossed the Alps into Switzerland by way of the Aprica, Julia and St Gotthard passes, continuing through Altdorf to Lucerne, going on to Geneva and Chamonix. The next stage of their tour took them down the Rhone Valley to Monte Carlo, after which came Lourdes, followed by Biarritz and San Sebastian in Northern Spain. To complete the tour they travelled north via Bordeaux and Tours to Trouville on the Normandy coast. They returned to Dieppe by way of Paris. The party arrived back in London in early October 1902, having covered 5,125 miles.

Throughout the entire course of this journey, apart from a few punctures, they experienced only one serious mishap. It occurred at the highest point of the St Gotthard pass, which was reached after a climb of 10½ miles made in a blinding snowstorm and howling gale. Whilst stopped at the top for a rest the petrol vapour froze in the carburettor. Their descent to Lake Lucerne had to be made by coasting for almost 10 miles until the frozen petrol thawed. The brakes on the car were crude by modern standards and without the slowing effect of engine compression the descent would have been extremely dangerous. When the party reached Hospenthal they were arrested for driving on a forbidden road and only released on payment of a fine of 30 francs.

# 5

# ARCTIC CIRCLE

On his return to Boston at the end of 1902, Glidden placed an order with Napier for an improved and more powerful car with greater space for both passengers and luggage. This was to be delivered to London ready for his return to the city in 1903. Not content with following the conventional tourist routes, he proposed to drive this car through northern Europe and Scandinavia, to within a short distance of the Arctic Circle.

Charles Thomas was waiting with the new car when Glidden returned to London. He is variously referred to by contemporary reports as 'that notable engineer from London', 'Mr Glidden's chauffeur' and 'Mr Glidden's mechanician'. He was obviously highly regarded by Glidden, with whom he continued to tour until 1907.

Glidden's new Napier was a 24hp model, with chain drive and 40in rear wheels, geared to a maximum speed of about 35mph. In common with all Napiers, it had electric ignition rather than the hot tube system. Selwyn Edge had encouraged Napier to make this change, despite there being some doubt as to its reliability.

Mulliners built the coachwork and upholstery to Glidden's own requirements, providing an especially large tonneau designed to accommodate a steamer trunk holding ten days' supply of clothing, many spare parts, a toolkit, inner tubes and tyres. The total weight of the car, with four passengers, was some 4,500lb.

Glidden planned first to tour Ireland and watch the Gordon Bennett Race, which was to be held at Athey, not far from Dublin. Glidden's interest was prompted by Selwyn Edge who, driving a Napier, had won the 1902 race and been automatically included as one of the three-man team allowed for the next running of the event. Napier drivers had also been chosen for the other two places.

If he expected to witness another Napier triumph Glidden was to be disappointed. During the race all three cars had problems: Edge experienced problems with his tyres, afterwards concluding that his vehicle was too heavy; the second suffered jammed steering and crashed; and the third ran wide on a corner, hit a barrier and broke its front wheels.

Petrol for the tank
and water for the
radiator. The water
was taken from
this village pump
somewhere in
Germany. (Author's
collection)

Verona's mayor gave special permission for the Napier to be taken into the city's Roman Coliseum. (*The Autocar*)

Waiting at a railway crossing somewhere in France. (Author's collection)

After touring Ireland Glidden intended to proceed, by way of Belfast, across the Irish Sea to Glasgow, and sail for Norway from one of Scotland's east-coast ports. The idea was to drive north to Trondheim and approach the Arctic Circle before returning through Sweden and Denmark to Northern Germany.

However, his plans were radically altered by the disasters of that year's Paris-Madrid road race, in which a number of fatal accidents occurred on the first day, 24 May 1903. The French government banned it two days later. The Norwegian authorities, fearing similar events, imposed severe restrictions on motor traffic. They required six days' notice for each stage of the route. Worse still, the car had to be led by a man on a horse. In order to avoid these difficulties Glidden decided to omit Norway altogether. He would sail from Hull to Copenhagen, then drive north through Sweden, returning by the same route.

Again, Glidden's preparation was detailed and thorough. Each day's drive was planned in advance, making good use of a set of 100 maps, as he described in his article in the *New England* magazine. In Sweden, arrangements were made for 15-gallon carboys of petrol to be stockpiled at strategic points along the proposed route. Entry and exit visas were obtained through the various US embassies and consular officials. Heavy reliance was placed on the *Baedeker Guides* and, in the UK, on R.E. Phillips's *Automobilist's Guide*.

On 25 June 1903, Mr and Mrs Glidden, accompanied by Charles Thomas, crossed by ferry from Liverpool to Belfast. The tour in Ireland amounted to 1,510 miles, from the Giant's Causeway in the north to Glengariff and Cork in the south, taking in the Gordon Bennett Race on the way. They then returned to Holyhead and crossed England to Hull. Here they boarded a ship to Copenhagen, where they were entertained by many of the city's notables including the American Consul and his wife. Their route then took them north to Helsingor and across the narrow straits to Helsingborg in Sweden. They drove next to Stockholm, during which they saw only five other cars. Glidden sent a postcard to the offices of *The Autocar* from Sundsvall dated 10 August 1903. At this point, they had been on the road for twenty-six days and had covered 2,800 miles.

They then travelled along the coast, through Skelleftea, to the town of Haparanda, on the present-day border between Sweden and Finland. The driving in Sweden was exceptionally hard going. The roads in the north of the country were empty and desolate. In 50 miles they might see just one person and the only other vehicles were mail wagons. Often the roads were no more than cart tracks, and there was an almost constant risk of running into a ditch. When this happened it was a case of tracking down a local farmer with a team of horses, or having to rely on their own muscle power to get it out. Yet even the remotest villages and towns had telephones so Glidden was able to call ahead to book hotels, check fuel supplies were in place and arrange for ferries.

The Napier was the first automobile ever seen in the more remote parts of the country. Every town and village gave them an enthusiastic welcome. People lined the roads and waved Swedish flags. Glidden responded by giving short 'spins' to people in the towns through which they passed.

Leaving Haparanda on their final stage, they came upon an old Finnish woman trudging along the road. With the aid of an interpreter Glidden asked where she was going.

'To my daughter's,' was the reply.

'How far is it?'

'15 miles.'

'When do you expect to arrive?'

'Tomorrow morning.'

Glidden took her into the car, wrapped her up warm, and in forty minutes she was at her daughter's home.

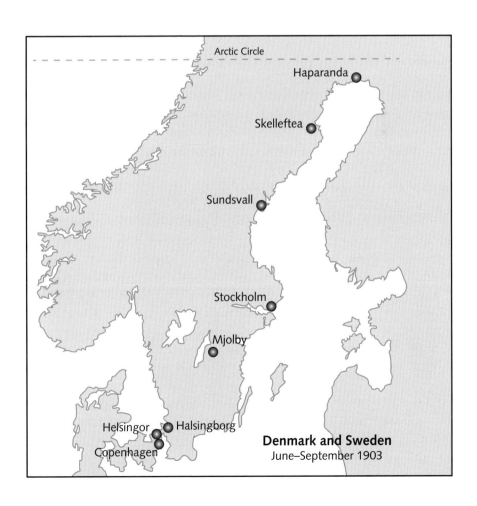

'God has put you in my way,' she said, followed by, 'I'm dying for a smoke.'
They bade farewell and left her puffing away on a large wooden pipe.

From Haparanda the local postmaster, their official witness, rode with the Napier on its journey northwards for a further 70 miles. Their average speed for this part of the trip was about 20mph, which was the norm for most of the tour.

Carrying the American and Swedish flags, in their British Napier car, the Gliddens and Charles Thomas crossed the Arctic Circle at 2 p.m. on 16 August 1903. They had completed the 700-mile drive north in just over five days.

They arrived back in Skellftea on 25 August and then travelled on to Stockholm. After a journey of 1,540 miles around Sweden, they travelled south to Hamburg and Berlin, after which the tour was broadly a repeat of their earlier European tour of 1902, though it took in some different cities. They finished in Holland, where they sailed from Rotterdam to Harwich. Then it was back to Liverpool for the voyage to Boston, leaving Charles Thomas to return the car to London for servicing by Napier.

Having completed a total of 6,670 miles and spent fifty-four days on the road, Glidden calculated driving time of 390 hours at an average of seven hours each day. The Napier had performed extremely well. There was only one major problem, a broken pump shaft, which took Charles Thomas half an hour to replace. They suffered only six punctures. Glidden attributed this high degree of reliability, in *New England* magazine, 'partly to the watchful care of Mr Charles

Arriving at Hull by ferry across the River Humber. (Author's collection)

The American Consul in Copenhagen pictured with his wife at the wheel.
(Author's collection)

Thomas, the London engineer who accompanied us, and partly to the excellent
construction of the car itself'.

By modern standards, the driving conditions they encountered were far from
ideal. This was the case even in England and France, where Glidden judged the
roads to be good. In Sweden, crossing rivers and small stretches of sea required
improvised ferries that were only intended for horse-drawn vehicles. Looking
back now, the route looks surprisingly convoluted, but one must remember that
this was often decided by the nature of the roads that were available, if indeed a
road existed at all. Glidden's original itinerary ran to about 4,500 miles and would
have taken him to within three degrees of his final goal. His actual route added
a further 2,000 miles and made him the first motorist to cross the Arctic Circle.

Having completed successful tours of northern and southern Europe, Glidden
decided to extend his horizons. He was planning new journeys that were to make
his Arctic Circle trip appear distinctly tame.

Landing on the quay at Halsingborg in Sweden. (Author's collection)

An overnight stop in Mjolby, halfway between Helsingborg and Stockholm. (Author's collection)

Ready to leave Stockholm for the Arctic Circle. (Author's collection)

On the road in more rural parts of Sweden north of Stockholm. Note the roadside telegraph poles. Despite the remoteness of the area, the telephone had already arrived. Glidden was able to phone ahead to book hotels, check fuel supplies were in place and arrange for ferries. (Author's collection)

Charles Thomas helps calm a horse unsettled by the Napier. (Author's collection)

A slight accident they did not avoid. (Author's collection)

Boarding a ferry somewhere in Sweden. (Author's collection)

An old Finnish woman.
(Author's collection)

# 6

# FROM SEA TO SHINING SEA

On 13 January 1904, Glidden announced that he would motor round the world, commencing from London in July. The journey was designed to last two years. Extensive correspondence was entered into, arranging for petrol supplies and, where necessary for safety, military escorts. Eight thousand miles of steamship passage was booked. The car would be the same Napier used to cross the Arctic Circle and Glidden would be accompanied throughout by his wife and Charles Thomas.

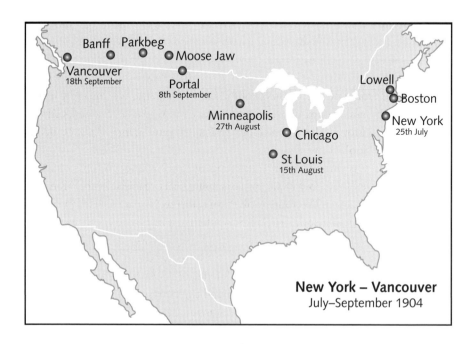

Banff   Parkbeg
Vancouver   ● Moose Jaw
18th September
Portal
8th September

Minneapolis
27th August

Chicago

St Louis
15th August

Lowell
Boston

New York
25th July

**New York – Vancouver**
July–September 1904

Glidden's original intention was to travel by way of North Africa, the Middle East, India and the Far East, before crossing the Pacific to America. However, by the time he reached London, his plans had changed because events in the USA offered him an opportunity for much favourable publicity.

Interviewed in his rooms at the Carlton Hotel by a journalist working for *The Autocar* magazine, he announced that he would first tour Britain's major cathedral cities, watch the elimination trials for the 1904 Gordon Bennett Race in the Isle of Man and then motor south to Hamburg in Germany for the race itself. Only after this would he commence the world tour, but in the reverse direction, shipping the car to America ready to cross the continent in September. He had also extended the route to take in the Pacific islands, Australia, New Zealand and parts of South East Asia and then North Africa. When the journalist queried the car's ability to tackle the sands of the desert Glidden's confident reply was, 'A Napier will go anywhere.'

Roads in the American mid-west and Rocky Mountains were extremely poor; using them would make it impossible to maintain the necessary schedule. The problem was solved in typical Glidden fashion by driving across the continent on the railroads.

Napier had experience of building railway vehicles. In 1903 they had built a petrol/electric rail car for the London & North Eastern Railway. During the winter, Napier altered the car's gearing and made special wheels for it. Trials proved successful and the wheels were shipped with the car to the USA. The car was also modified in other ways: it was given a new hydraulic governor and fitted with the most recent high-tension ignition system with an advance and retard lever on the centre of the steering wheel.

Despite his wealth and influence not all railroads welcomed Glidden's approaches. 'I would not have you on our tracks at any price,' was the reply he got from one indignant company president. Luckily the Canadian Pacific Railroad and its US extension – The Minneapolis, St Paul & Sault Sainte Marie Railroad, known as 'The Soo' – were willing.

The Napier was shipped from Southampton on 24 June 1904. On 25 July Glidden's party left New York as part of a reliability trial organised by the American Automobile Association. The route took them north to Niagara Falls, then west to Chicago before turning south to St Louis where, to mark the centenary of the Louisiana Purchase, the World's Fair and Olympic Games were being held.

Although roads in upper New York State were the worst they had yet travelled over, they arrived in St Louis on the scheduled date, 15 August. The 16th was the anniversary of their Arctic Circle crossing and the Napier was put on display in the Transportation Pavilion. The only British-built car in the fair, it drew much attention. The car was much admired until its rail wheels were fitted, whereupon some railroad men, who were there exhibiting a locomotive, said the car would

Glidden displaying the Napier in front of the Transportation Pavilion at the St Louis World's Fair just after the original railway wheels had been fitted. Note how shallow their flanges are and that they do not extend to the outer edge of the rails. (Author's collection / *The Autocar*)

jump the track when passing over points because the wheel rims were too narrow and their flanges too shallow. A trial was arranged and the railroad men were proved correct. The wheels therefore were sent to workshops in Pennsylvania for modification, after which they were forwarded to Minneapolis. Meanwhile the car was sent by rail to Chicago. (Since Chicago's longitude is to the east of St Louis no westward progress was made other than by the Napier's own power.)

From Chicago they drove north to Milwaukee, then 389 miles west to La Crosse on the Mississippi. It was harvest time and Wisconsin was a rich agricultural state so there were many farm wagons on the road. The Napier was the first car that the farmers had ever seen, and they were continually obliged to pull over and switch off the engine so that frightened horses could be calmed and led past. Most of the farmers took it in good humour but some gave vent to their feelings with more robust language.

Crossing the Mississippi into Minnesota, they travelled over empty prairie. In a day's run of twelve hours they passed neither house nor person. Becoming hungry, and with nowhere to buy a meal, Mr Glidden shot a number of wild birds which they cooked over a small fire and eat by the roadside. 'I do not know what kind of birds they were,' said Mr Glidden later, 'but I do know that they were good eating to a hungry mobile party.'

They arrived in Minneapolis on 27 August. During the following week Charles Thomas gave the car a complete overhaul after which the modified rail wheels were fitted and the steering wheel clamped at dead centre; on rails only the accelerator, brake and gear lever were needed.

On 3 September a 75-mile test run was made on the Soo's tracks. E. Pennington, second vice-president and general manager; T.A. Fogue, master mechanic; and four other railroad officials went with them.

The car crossed over points in the marshalling yard without any problems and performed well on gradients. A speed of 60mph was safely achieved on a straight and level section of the main line, although the wheel bearings warmed up slightly.

Leaving Minneapolis. Company vice-president E. Pennington and master mechanic T.A. Fogue sit behind Mr and Mrs Glidden. Conductor Joseph E. Horne is to the right of the lady waving the Stars and Stripes. (Author's collection)

Stopping to let an overheated axle box cool down. (Author's collection)

The car had to carry all the safety and signalling equipment found on a normal train: fire extinguisher, sand box, red flag, red lantern, detonators, red fire and other fireworks. Glidden also carried a portable telegraphy set which, in case of need, could be connected to the track side wires.

On the appointed day, Sunday 4 September, at 9.30 a.m., the Napier was backed down from the workshops to the station, and positioned ready to follow a scheduled express. Other stations along the line were notified of their coming. Conductor Joseph E. Horne took charge, his orders controlling the movement of the car in accordance with instructions issued by the train dispatchers.

They ran as a separate section of a nine-carriage express drawn by *Big Mogul* No. 508. Crowds of people, including railroad officials, employees, and many Minneapolis friends, cheered them on their way. The weather was cool and bracing as the express train pulled out of the station.

'Now we are off,' said Conductor Horne. On went the ignition. At first the Napier's driving wheels slipped on the highly polished rail, but, finally taking hold, the car moved away. Glidden accelerated and at one point they caught sight of the express but soon their new wheel bearings began to overheat and they were forced to stop and let them cool. This bothered them for three days, until the bearings were properly run in.

Conductor Horne ensured safe progress, warning Glidden of places where men were at work maintaining the permanent way or calling attention to level crossings.

The Napier had no regular stopping places and their only halts were for fuel, which had been sent ahead, to pass other trains or receive new orders.

One hundred and sixty miles from Minneapolis they reached Elbow Lake, soon after entering the great wheat-growing expanses of North Dakota. Further north there were fields of flax and fruit orchards. Another 236 miles brought them to Portal on the Canadian border, which they reached on 7 September.

The following morning Conductor Edgar H. Cooke, of the Canadian Pacific Railway, took charge for the 168 miles to the main line at Moose Jaw. They left Portal at 9 a.m., ten minutes ahead of an express, and by the time they arrived at Moose Jaw they had increased this to one hour ahead.

From Moose Jaw to Calgary was 500 miles of open prairie over which the wind blew unchecked. One day it was so strong that speed had to be reduced to 30mph and, for the sake of comfort, Mrs Glidden was compelled to sit low down in the tonneau.

Stopping at Parkbeg, a small prairie station in Saskatchewan west of Moose Jaw. (Author's collection)

Taking a siding to pass an oncoming train. (Author's collection)

Arriving in Vancouver. Conductor Alexander B. Forrest sits beside Charles Thomas at the rear of the car. The ship in the background is SS *Empress of India*. (Author's collection)

The Autocar. ADVERTISEMENTS. October 22nd, 1904. 3

# NAPIER
## FASTER THAN EXPRESS TRAINS.

"Runs perfectly smooth at sixty miles per hour, without a moment's delay."

Banff Springs Hotel,
Banff, Canada,
Sept. 11th, 1904.

Dear Mr. Edge,

You cannot realise what a wonderful drive I am having on the railroad tracks. My car runs perfectly sixty miles per hour as smooth as could be desired, in fact perfectly smooth. We lead the express trains—start after them and catch up.

Best I could do on road is forty miles per hour, but on track sixty—not a moment's delay. Show this to Napier.

Best wishes,
Yours very truly,
(Signed) CHAS. GLIDDEN.

## Mr. Glidden has already passed his 18,000th mile.

S. F. Edge, Ltd.,

14, New Burlington Street,
London, W.

### NO OTHER CAR IN EITHER HEMISPHERE HOLDS SUCH AN ENVIABLE RECORD.

Advertisement for S.F. Edge Ltd illustrating how Edge used Glidden's journeys to promote his business. (*The Autocar*)

They frequently caught slower freight trains, which they were obliged to follow to a siding before they could overtake.

After Medicine Hat they passed many Native American villages whose people turned out to watch and wave. From Calgary they were again made the second section of an express for an 82-mile run up steep mountain grades to Banff. They followed the express so closely that they were able to talk to passengers on the platform of the rear carriage.

At Laggan, in the Rockies, Conductor Alexander B. Forrest assumed control, remaining with them all the way to Vancouver. The Rocky Mountain scenery was wonderful. They drove among the snow-capped peaks, rounding curves on high trestles, in and out of dark rocky tunnels and snow sheds, alongside rushing streams and past roaring waterfalls.

They reached the summit of Kicking Horse Pass without any trouble and the steep descent of 1,140ft in 7 miles was made without the use of brakes, the momentum of the car being checked by cylinder compression. Crossing over the pass the temperature fell to -10°F so, fearing they might skid on icy rails, they followed close behind a passenger train.

Leaving the Rockies, they tackled the grades leading over the Selkirk Range. At Notch Hill a train dispatcher, thinking to tease them, asked if they needed an extra locomotive to help push them up. Glidden politely refused the offer, put the car in gear and to the utter amazement of all the railroad men on that section of track, reached the summit of the climb two hours faster than the prestigious *Imperial Express*.

The Napier reached the Vancouver terminus of the Canadian Pacific at 2 p.m. on 18 September 1904. Two thousand people lined the station platform, cheering loudly as the Napier came to its final stop – they had succeeded in crossing the American continent 'from sea to shining sea'.

The following day Mr and Mrs Glidden, together with Charles Thomas, left Vancouver east-bound on the CPR for Boston, where they arrived on the evening of the 25th. Glidden was intending to ship the car to Australia, calling at Hawaii, Fiji and New Zealand on the way, but a delay of two months was necessary in order to arrive during January, at the height of the southern hemisphere summer. In New Zealand he hoped to match the record for taking a car as far north as possible by motoring as far south as possible.

Glidden spent the intervening months giving lectures on his journeys to date. He also commissioned a magnificent silver trophy from Tiffany of New York which he presented to the American Automobile Association. It was to be awarded annually for the most successful car tour anywhere in the USA or Canada. Charles Thomas spent the time working in Napier's Boston salesroom.

# 7

# ACROSS THE PACIFIC

Returning to Vancouver, Charles Thomas prepared the Napier for a long sea voyage as deck cargo. All metal parts were greased and the car was swung to the aft bulkhead of SS *Moana*, securely lashed and covered with a tarpaulin. They sailed from Vancouver at 1.47 p.m. on Friday, 9 December 1904. Their course took them south, along the eastern coast of Vancouver Island to the provincial capital of Victoria, where the ship took on mail. After that it passed through the Straits of Juan de Fuca, rounded Cape Flattery and set a south-westerly course for Hawaii.

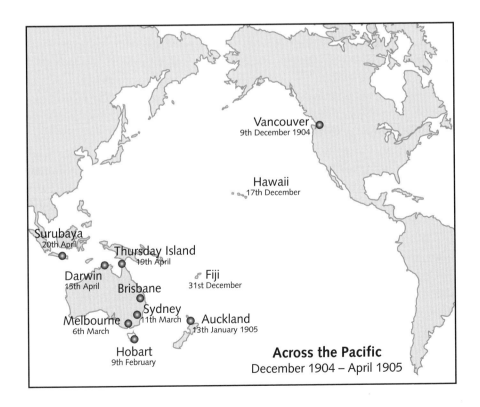

Vancouver
9th December 1904

Hawaii
17th December

Surubaya
20th April

Thursday Island
19th April

Darwin
15th April

Brisbane

Fiji
31st December

Sydney
11th March

Auckland
13th January 1905

Melbourne
6th March

Hobart
9th February

**Across the Pacific**
December 1904 – April 1905

The first five days were very rough and stormy. Waves broke over the ship, flooding Glidden's first-class stateroom and forcing them to a drier cabin on a lower deck where they remained for two days, suffering from seasickness. When matters were at their worst the stewardess came into the cabin. Paying no attention to their distress she read out the ship's menu, listing such dishes as chicken liver sauté and stewed kidneys, before they managed to call a halt.

Big seas swept over the Napier, drenching unprotected parts, but doing no damage except removing some paint and deflating two tyres. On the eighth day they crossed the Tropic of Cancer and the sea grew calmer.

They were completely surprised by a ship's fire drill, during which a ship's steward carried their five cases of gasoline to the aft deck and pretended to throw them into the sea.

At six o'clock on Saturday 17 December, eight days after leaving Vancouver, they had their first glimpse of Hawaii. An hour and a half later the ship was at the quayside. The Captain promised them three hours' shore time and, after Charles Thomas had put the Napier in running order, it was craned onto the dockside. Petrol was available at 30 cents a gallon and they were soon on their way, calling on the US Governor before driving to the summit of the Palli, from where they enjoyed a fine view of the island. Realising they had almost used up their three hours, they hurried back to the *Moana*, breaking the speed limit as they did so but without drawing the attention of the local police.

Exactly on time, the Napier was placed back on board and the ship resumed her voyage. They crossed the equator at 5.37 p.m. on Wednesday 21 December. On the 25th they were at fifteen degrees south. Coincidentally they crossed the International Date Line and the Captain teased them by announcing that it was now 26 December and that Christmas had been missed. Despite this, carols were sung and seasonal greetings exchanged. Five lady passengers decorated the ship's saloon with the Union Jack while Mr and Mrs Glidden made sure the Stars and Stripes they were carrying round the world was also on display. The captain cut a Christmas pudding in which gifts were concealed. The day ended with the passengers entertaining the crew with a concert after which all the Britons on board sang 'God Save the King' before everyone retired to their bunks.

The last day of 1904 saw them in Suva, the capital of Fiji. The Napier was put ashore and they drove to a hotel owned and run by a Mrs Macdonald, a Scots lady who had made her home in Fiji. It was the first car ever seen on the island and attracted great attention. Crowds of Fijians followed the car, completely surrounding it more than 100 deep. They nicknamed it 'the God of Fire', 'the Father of all Devils' and 'the Boat on the Road'.

That night Glidden took advantage of Fiji's position on the edge of the International Date Line to exercise his fondness for being the first person in the world to perform some remarkable deed. The fact that it involved telegraphy,

Glidden poses with the King of Fiji. (Author's collection)

his particular area of expertise, only added to his sense of satisfaction. At exactly one second after midnight he sent a telegram wishing 'Happy New Year to the Globe and automobilists everywhere'. Having made special arrangements with the companies that operated the transoceanic cables, and allowing for the seventeen-hour time difference, his message took just two and a half minutes to travel 8,500 miles and reach the offices of the *Boston Globe*. The story of how Glidden had sent the first telegraphic greeting of the New Year took up most of that day's front page.

Whilst on Fiji Glidden favoured many people, islanders as well as Europeans, with a ride in the Napier; among them was Fiji's King, *Ratu Penal a Kadavu Levu Roko Tui Tailevu* (Principal Chief Penaia Kadavu Reverenced King of Great Country). He was a young man, educated in Sydney and fluent in English, who possessed some knowledge of motor cars, although this was the first he had ever seen. He enquired about the car's top speed, paid particular attention to the working of the machinery and was allowed to drive it, at moderate speed, in a safe open area. Sailing schedules compelled a disappointed Glidden to refuse the King's invitation to stay at the royal home.

They also gave a ride to the King's sister, Princess Adi Cakobau, whom they met one evening as she walked along Suva's promenade. Although she spoke no

A Fijian Princess sits beside Mr Glidden with Mrs Glidden standing behind her. Mrs MacDonald, proprietor of the hotel at which they stayed, stands behind Mr Glidden. (Author's collection / *The Autocar*)

English, she halted and by means of an interpreter was presented to the Gliddens, accepting an invitation to ride the next day. At the start of the ride she was a little apprehensive but quickly became accustomed to the car and very much enjoyed the experience.

One morning they met Cannibal Tom coming along the road. He was supposed to have taken part in forty-eight cannibal feasts. Accepting a shilling, he

Cannibal Tom. (Author's
collection)

Led by their European
officer, native Fijian
police parade in front
of the Napier. (Author's
collection / *The Autocar*)

posed for his photograph and remarked that the corpulent Mr Glidden would be fine eating.

The tropical climate of Fiji caused some concern. In the extreme heat their supply of petrol threatened to evaporate and the Napier's tyres and wooden wheel spokes needed to be kept damp.

At midnight on 6 January 1905 the car was loaded onto the deck of the Union Steamship Company's *Navua*, bound for Auckland. A ten-point drop of the barometer indicated the approach of a typhoon and the *Navua* anchored in the harbour to wait out the storm. After seven hours the wind decreased and the ship sailed at 1.47 p.m. the following day.

They were 600 miles from land when fire was discovered in a coal bunker. Anxious passengers feared they would have to take to the lifeboats in an area of the ocean where there was little prospect of rescue. The captain, however, remained calm. A hose was passed into the bunker, water pumped in and the fire extinguished.

# 8

# NEW ZEALAND

Landing in Auckland, Glidden's party were welcomed by members of the local Automobile Association who gave them guided tours of the spectacular volcanic scenery. Glidden was guest of honour at a dinner held in the city's Grand Hotel, where he delivered a talk on his travels to date.

They left the city at 10.30 a.m. on Friday 13 January, intending to be the first to drive the length of both North and South Islands. The road was rough, bumpy and dangerous, with sections of heavy clay which would have been impassable in the wet but fortunately the day was dry and sunny. After 65 miles they passed through the Taupiri Gorge and came to the Waikato River, which they crossed via a ford. There were many small fords to cross that day, and, due to the uncertain

Wellington, New Zealand. (Author's collection)

condition of the stream beds, they carried block and tackle in case the car became trapped. The day's drive ended at Hamilton, after they had covered a distance of 100 miles in six hours.

The next morning they made an early start and, and after considerable shaking up on bad roads, reached Rotorua ahead of a storm that threatened to make the roads impassable. Their overnight stop was in a small hotel so crowded that the Gliddens had to sleep on a cot in the parlour whilst Charles Thomas slept on the billiard table.

The following day they toured the geysers, which Glidden thought comparable to those of Yellowstone Park in Wyoming. Their guide was an educated, English-speaking Maori girl named Maggie who introduced them to her aunts and uncles in the village of Whakarewerawera.

They attended a Sunday service held in the village's Catholic church, and were impressed by the Maoris in their best costumes and by the quality of the hymn singing. After church they drove the car into the village. Some of the Maoris were reluctant to be photographed, believing that the camera might steal part of their life force. However, Maggie persuaded them otherwise and photographs were taken.

On 16 January they drove 110 miles to Tarawera on the Waipunga River, crossing the hard, baked earth of the Rununga Plain, and ascended the Ahimanaya Mountains.

Maoris gather by the car in their village near Rotorua. (Author's collection)

A Maori chief, wearing a cloak of kiwi feathers, at the wheel of the Napier. Beside him is their guide Maggie. (Author's collection)

The next morning they made an early start for the journey along the east coast, which involved driving over what Glidden described as the most difficult and dangerous mountain road in the world, consisting of 50 miles of severe climbs and descents, passing around eight mountain peaks. In some places the road was cut out of the mountain side with a 1,500-foot drop only feet away to the side. They crossed several rivers at speed, the hot engine throwing up clouds of steam.

At the top of the highest pass they met a massive flock of 4,000 sheep and so were obliged to abandon the car and hide in the bushes whilst they passed. Loose horses on the road also caused trouble: they ran ahead for miles, throwing up clouds of dust. One plunged to its death over a precipice.

On Thursday 19 January they drove 170 miles from Napier to Masterton, continuing the following day to Wellington, where the local manager of the New Zealand tourist service handed Glidden a report on the condition of the roads in South Island. He had planned on crossing the Cook Straits and then driving the entire length of South Island; however, conditions in the Marlborough district of South Island were very bad. Snow was melting from the Southern Alps, threatening to flood the gorges through which they would have to pass.

On Monday 23 January they drove around the harbour of Wellington and looked across Cook Straits to the snow-capped ranges of South Island. The

Auckland
13th January 1905

Hamilton

Rotorua

Tarawera
16th January 1905

Napier
19th January 1905

Masterton

Wellington
23rd January 1905

Christchurch
28th January 1905

Timaru

Dunedin

Bluff →  Invercargill
5th February 1905   31st January 1905

**New Zealand**
January – February 1905

decision was made to bypass the difficult section and so a steamer was booked for an overnight passage to Christchurch, 150 miles further down the east coast of South Island. The cost of this short voyage annoyed Glidden. It was $26.75 for one night's passage compared with $30 for the entire journey from Vancouver to Auckland.

Glidden was very gratified by the reception given him in Christchurch. He addressed members of the City's Automobile Club on the subject of his world tour and the City Council consulted him about the establishment of a speed limit. He was also taken on inspection tours of refrigeration plants where New

Passing a mail coach. Charles Thomas calms a team of nervous horses. (Author's collection)

Fording a river on the way to the town of Napier. The bare trees are the result of a forest fire. (Author's collection)

The hotel at Tarawera between Rotorua and the town of Napier. (Author's collection)

Halting at the top of the Rimatuku Pass. (Author's collection)

Zealand mutton was frozen for shipment to Britain. Everywhere he went Glidden took particular interest in how European colonists were establishing trade and industry. In his letters to the *Boston Globe* he particularly took note of places where American companies were involved or where opportunities existed for them to become involved.

South of Christchurch the roads were reported to be good, but this proved to be false. The roads were of soft clay with many loose stones and there were at least 100 streams to be forded. Inland, immense avalanches of snow were falling into the valleys, at first blocking streams, but then, as they melted, suddenly increasing the flow to dangerous levels at times that could not be predicted.

They left the city on 28 January for the drive to Dunedin. The drive took two days and there was heavy rain. Several long detours were necessary to find fords that were shallow enough to cross. At Cooper's Creek the ford was 50ft wide with 3ft of rushing water. Halfway across, water filled the exhaust and the engine stalled. Luckily some locals fetched a horse and they were pulled to dry land.

When they did come to a river crossed by a bridge it was completely blocked by a flock of 5,000 sheep. Slowly, helped by the shepherds and their dogs, they managed to pass.

As in rural parts of the USA there were many horse-drawn wagons, as well as mail coaches. Unlike their American counterparts, New Zealand farmers were not angered by the effect of the car upon their horses but were rather embarrassed at their own apparent lack of skill in controlling their animals. Glidden showed consideration by stopping the car whenever there was a problem and Charles Thomas's experience with his father's horse buses enabled him to calm the frightened creatures and lead them past.

Their overnight stop was in Timaru, a town of 5,000 people. The next morning they continued on through the sea port of Oamaru, 150 miles from Christchurch, after which there where steep climbs over several mountain ranges until they reached Dunedin, where they were greeted by an escort of local motorists.

Leaving Dunedin on the morning of 31 January, they drove to Invercargill over 100 miles of the best roads in the country and 50 miles of the worst. For 8 miles they ran alongside the Southland Express, spoke with the engineer and waved to the passengers. Eventually a herd of sheep blocked the way and the train disappeared into the distance.

On 5 February 1905 they drove from Invercargill to Bluff, 17 miles further south, over a rough bumpy road, and through a mile of deep sand which made progress difficult. For 5 miles the way was along cliffs, high on a rocky coastline.

Finally they came to a halt, with the Straits of Foveaux to their left, across which Stewart Island was visible. They were as far south as it was then possible to drive a car.

# 9

# ADVENTURES DOWN UNDER

The day after reaching their southern-most point of New Zealand, the Napier, along with Glidden, his wife and Thomas, was loaded aboard SS *Monowai* and they sailed the same evening. The crossing of the Tasman Sea was uneventful, other than the fact that for much of the way the ship was followed by albatross.

At 5 p.m. on 9 February *Monowai* drew alongside the wharf at Hobart, Tasmania, and the motor car was unloaded without incident. Again Glidden was gratified by the reception granted him by local dignitaries. The president of the Tasmania Tourist Association, Senator the Hon. Henry Dobson, a former Premier of Tasmania, welcomed him and insisted on signing a $1,200 bond guaranteeing

Launceston, Tasmania. (Author's collection)

that the car would be taken out of the Commonwealth within twelve months, which saved the annoyance of making a special deposit in Tasmanian funds which might then be reclaimed in Queensland less commission and tax.

A conference was being held in Hobart and Glidden was invited to a series of social occasions at which he met senior government ministers – including the Prime Minister of Australia, the Right Hon. G.H. Reid KC and the Hon. J.W. Evans, Premier of Tasmania, to whom he gave a ceremonious ride in the car.

He toured 462 miles round the island, taking approving note of the development of European colonisation and commercial development, the fruit growing, timber and gold mining industries. He was impressed by the luxuriant vegetation, especially the ferns, but disconcerted by the number of poisonous reptiles and insects.

The speed at which Tasmanians did business was frustrating. Any New York bank would accept Glidden's letter of credit but in Hobart he was obliged to try three banks before he found one that, as a special favour and for a small fee, would do so. At the post office he stood in line for ten minutes to buy stamps and then the clerk refused to issue the particular values he wanted.

On the road to Ballarat. (Author's collection)

A lunch stop somewhere between Bendigo and Melbourne. (Author's collection)

Aborigines of the Coranderrk Reserve with their superintendent, Rev. Joseph Shaw. (Author's collection)

A sea passage from Hobart took them to Melbourne, where they arrived on 18 February and received the, by now, customary reception from the members of the local Automobile Club. Glidden was disappointed to discover that none of the Australian newspapers printed New York or London stock market quotations. He compensated for this by driving the 205 miles west to Hamilton, passing many enormous sheep stations on the way. He then returned to Melbourne by way of the gold mining towns of Ballarat and Bendigo. In the days of the Australian Gold Rush these had been rowdy and rebellious mining camps but were now peaceful communities with well-laid-out roads, brick buildings and parks planted with flowers.

They stopped at the Aboriginal reserve of Coranderrk, 50 miles east of Melbourne, where they were given a friendly welcome by its superintendent, Rev. Joseph Shaw. The Aborigines in general were rather shy about being photographed, but after a party of children were taken for a ride there was no more difficulty.

They left Melbourne at six o'clock on Monday 6 March for the drive to Sydney, 571 miles away. The first 50 miles of road was fair but then they came to remote bush country where the road was full of deep potholes, dust and sand. Many bridges had been destroyed by bush fires which made it difficult to cross ravines. Settlements were scarce and widely separated. One day they were offered lunch by an engineer in his lonely camp where he was inspecting the Melbourne–Sydney telegraph line.

In the small town of Gupdagai, where they stopped for the night, a tense situation had developed. Fearing for his life, the manager of a local cattle station had taken refuge in the same hotel as the motorists. He had caught two local men stealing his stock. They had been arrested and were to be put on trial. Public sympathy was very much in favour of the rustlers and everybody in town was carrying guns.

Leaving town the following morning, Glidden and his party were hailed by a local newspaper reporter wanting to know where they were going. Told they were bound round the world the reporter's response was, 'O yes, like the Yankee who drove his car on the railway lines.'

On 11 March they were escorted into Sydney by thirty motor vehicles, and speeches of welcome were given by leading members of the city's Automobile Club. In reply Mr Glidden thanked them for the courtesy shown him and his wife. Mrs Glidden was presented with a bouquet in the form of a motor-wheel, and the president of the club decorated Mr Glidden with the badge of the Automobile Club of Australia. They stayed in Sydney for more than a week, during which time they were entertained at a number of social functions and went for a cruise in the harbour on a petrol-driven launch.

They considered driving north to Brisbane but, hearing of bad roads, dengue fever and several cases of plague, decided against it and so sailed aboard the steamer *Airlee* on 1 April, bound for Surabaya in Java. The *Airlee* was a small single-screw ship of 2,300 tons with passenger cabins way astern over the propeller shaft. She

SS *Airlee*. (Author's collection)

was commanded by a Captain Williams and also carried a Torres Strait pilot who took command at night, especially whilst passing inside the Great Barrier Reef.

They sailed down Sydney Harbour, meeting heavy seas as they passed between the North and South Heads. The first two days of the voyage were rough and there was a continuous deluge of rain which kept all the passengers in their berths. The ship pitched and rolled, her hull creaking and groaning. At one point Glidden was rolled completely out of his bunk and large amounts of crockery were smashed in the galley and mess room.

The cargo, a mixture of lead, iron, lumber and coal, held the ship well down in the water and breaking waves flooded the decks to a depth of 4ft. The water hardly had time to drain off before another wave came aboard. It was impossible to keep their staterooms dry.

In the evening of the second day the ship anchored off Brisbane, and it was a great relief to rest in calm waters for a few hours. They did not go ashore as one half of Brisbane's population was down with the dengue fever, and there were also several cases of bubonic plague.

The ship had been thoroughly fumigated before leaving Sydney; nevertheless, cockroaches 3 inches long, mosquitoes the size of wasps and hundreds of brown biting ants infested the staterooms, and rats ran over the faces of the passengers at night.

Leaving Brisbane, the ship sailed north in waters protected by the Great Barrier Reef. On some of the small islands Aborigines could be seen collecting sea cucumbers. Known as trepang, they were valued at $1,000 per ton and exported to China where they were considered a great delicacy. Many of the islands held large colonies of nesting sea birds.

Nine days after leaving Sydney they cleared the Torres Straits and came to port in Thursday Island. No sooner was the ship alongside the wharf than three of the passengers were taken ashore, suffering from dengue fever.

Thursday was famous for pearl diving and had a large population of many nationalities, European, Malay and Chinese, who crowded the wharf to stare at the car. Two days were spent transferring cargo and then *Airlee* sailed across the Gulf of Carpentaria, arriving in Darwin on 15 April.

To check that it had suffered no harm from the soaking received during the rough weather just north of Sydney, the car was started up and run back and forth along the ship's deck, and the town's inhabitants thronged to see it. There was neither time nor sufficient roads to justify putting it ashore.

They then crossed the Timor Sea, among islands where the great powers competed for sovereignty. The Russo-Japanese War was at its height and the Battle of Tsushima was yet to be fought. The ship's cargo might have been considered contraband of war and so there was a risk of Japanese gun-boats searching the ship, but in the event they crossed unhindered.

Their passage through the Madura Straits to Surabaya was a pleasant end to a long voyage. On the right was the mountainous island of Madura and on the left the main coast of Java. Volcanoes 11,000ft high belched smoke and lava while towns and villages clustered at their base.

Twenty days after leaving Sydney they made port in Surabaya. The motor car was lowered to a lighter and they went ashore in a native sampan. The thermometer registered 90°F and hardly a breath of the hot, humid air was stirring.

# 10

# JAVA, SINGAPORE AND A WEDDING

The Dutch authorities in Surabaya, though polite, disapproved of the car and there were many bureaucratic delays before entry was granted. The car was closely inspected by the Governor General's chief railway engineer, who certified it to be mechanically sound. Glidden's ability to drive carefully and considerately was also certified. A deposit of £30 had to be paid as a guarantee of his financial worth and good faith, after which the Post Office issued permits for the three members of the party to stay in Java for six months. It took them three days of form-filling before all the formalities were completed.

On the road in Java. (Author's collection)

They had some problems finding a reliable guide and interpreter and only succeeded on the third attempt. On Monday 24 April they set out for Jogjakarta on the south coast of the island. The previous night heavy rain had fallen and streams had burst their banks, flooding villages and roads. In some places they were forced to hire water buffalo to pull the car from the floods, and several long detours were needed to find bridges across wide rivers, as there were no river craft large enough to trust as a ferry.

In some of the muddy streams they saw crocodiles and there were peacocks in the dense forests. Troops of monkeys patrolled the road and pelted them with coconuts and broken branches but scampered away at the sound of the horn.

Java was heavily populated and the roads, apart from river crossings, were good – though crowded with pedestrians and carts. Progress was slow and they had to make continual use of their horn. Since the people went barefoot, the roads were kept clear of stones and all sharp objects so there was less fear of a puncture than anywhere else they had driven.

Arriving in Jogjakarta, Glidden sought and was granted an audience with the Sultan of Java. There was a delay of one day, though, because it was a Friday, the Islamic holy day, so at eleven o'clock on the Saturday they drove to the palace and were received with full eastern court ceremony, including the playing of a gamelan orchestra which to Glidden's ears sounded 'peculiar'. When the Sultan entered the audience chamber his courtiers waddled along behind him, squatting

Filling up with water from a roadside well. (Author's collection)

on their heels. His daughters performed a court dance lasting for an hour and a half, after which the Sultan, together with the bearer of his golden ceremonial umbrella, three of his wives, one of his daughters and the Dutch Assistant Resident, were crammed into the Napier and taken for a ride. The car kept to walking pace so that a mounted bodyguard could keep station.

From Jogjakarta they drove to Semarang on the north coast of the island, stopping to see the ancient Buddhist temples at Barabodur. From Semarang it was a three-day drive west along the coast to Batavia (now called Jakarta) where they arrived on Friday 5 May.

Three miles below the city at Tanjong Priok, 'Corner of the Port', the motor car was placed on the small Dutch steamer *de Carpentier* and they sailed for Singapore the following day. The voyage lasted forty hours, during which two boxes of incense were kept continually burning to sweeten the air against unpleasant odours coming from the steerage compartment, which was occupied by 200 Chinese coolies, and 100 live pigs packed into crates.

Singapore was a free port so there was no customs examination and the Standard Oil Company of New York was on hand to supply petrol at 40 cents a gallon. After unloading the car Glidden simply took his seat at the wheel and drove to the Raffles Hotel, whilst their luggage followed behind in a bullock cart.

Despite its fame, Glidden did not have a high opinion of the Raffles; he considered the menu poor and its rooms dingy. The Chinese waiters spoke very little English and did not understand his sign language.

Another annoyance was the need to apply for a permit to take photographs. This was granted, provided that none were taken of military fortifications.

Glidden was, however, taken with the thriving commerce of Singapore and by the fact that several of his fellow Boston businessmen had interests in the tin mines of nearby Malaya.

It was commerce that attracted people of many races and differing religions to the island. Visiting a Hindu temple, Glidden nearly blundered across the sacred threshold into the Holy of Holies. This would have made the entire temple ritually impure but a quick-thinking priest pulled him back in time and then preceded him everywhere he went whilst he inspected other parts of the building.

Leaving the car on the island, they were entertained by the Sultan of Johore, who sent his personal motor launch across the straits to collect them. They ate lunch off a solid gold dinner service and in the course of conversation learned that the Sultan had himself just purchased a 90hp motor car.

At this point the 1904–05 tour ended. The car was shipped back to London on a freight steamer whilst Mr and Mrs Glidden took passage aboard the German-Lloyd liner SS *Preussen* bound for Naples, after which they travelled by train to Southampton, sailing from there to New York. Among the *Preussen's* other passengers were a number of dejected Russian officers, brought low by news of the Battle of Tsushima and their nation's defeat at the hands of the Japanese.

Also aboard were colonial officials returning to Europe with their families. The children, having been born and raised in the Tropics, were used to going barefoot, but when the ship passed through the Suez Canal the weather grew much cooler and, for the first time, the children were obliged to wear shoes. Some ran about in excitement, but for others the experience was painful and brought tears.

Arriving back in England, Charles Thomas saw to the overhaul and refurbishment of the Napier at the company's works in Acton, including re-upholstering and re-painting.

Meanwhile Napier's, with the encouragement of S.F. Edge, had become involved in power-boat racing. They built two craft – *Napier* and *Napier II* – which were entered in a race from Boulogne to Folkestone and back organised by the Automobile Club de France. *Napier II* was owned by Lord Howard de Walden and Charles Thomas acted as his engineer for the race. *Napier* suffered from mechanical problems during the race and had to retire, but *Napier II* battled it out with a French boat named *Rapiere*. Approaching the finish off Boulogne, *Napier II* held a narrow lead when the crew mistook the course and passed the wrong side of a buoy. This cost them a victory which otherwise seemed certain; nevertheless Charles Thomas was awarded a bronze medal by the organisers.

On 9 October 1905 he married Laura May Brooke at a registry office in Bitterne, Southampton. One wedding gift was a handsome engraved silver tea-set from S.F. Edge. That evening the newlyweds left Southampton by steamer for Le Havre, going for a week's honeymoon in Paris. The reason for the registry office may have been Glidden's decision to embark on a second tour at the end of the month. There was simply not enough time for the bans to be called and a church ceremony arranged.

# 11

# INDIA: BOMBAY AND THE DECCAN

In Europe and North America and even parts of Asia, the Napier had never been completely beyond the reach of aid, should mechanical failure have made it necessary, but now Glidden was planning journeys in regions where technical assistance would be more distant and problematic. To overcome this difficulty he had five crates built to his own specification.

Safe arrival in Poona after driving over the Western Ghats. (Author's collection / *The Autocar / Boston Sunday Globe*)

Storms in the North Pacific had shown that shipping the Napier as unprotected deck cargo put it at risk and so the first crate was designed for the car itself. The second contained extra tyres and inner tubes in addition to those carried on the car. The third held a spare engine shaft and a full set of springs. Other spare parts, not carried on the car, were in the fourth, while the fifth was for the railroad wheels. From now on these crates were sent in advance of the car, to be held at major ports or railroad centres no more than a week's travel from wherever they might be. Glidden also had an arrangement with Eastman Kodak for a monthly supply of photographic film to be sent from Rochester, New York, to agreed points on his intended route.

On 31 October 1905 he gave a press conference at the Carlton Hotel in London in which he announced that, instead of continuing the world tour westwards, he would be returning to the east. The Napier was crated up and Charles Thomas supervised its shipment to Bombay (now Mumbai) on board SS *Delta*. Mr and Mrs Glidden did not accompany the car but went by rail to Marseilles where they embarked on the maiden voyage of P&O's *Mooltan*, sailing on 10 November. They arrived in Bombay on the 24th to find the car held in customs. Before it could be released a deposit of $175 had to be paid as a guarantee that it would not be sold in the country and that it would be taken out after three months.

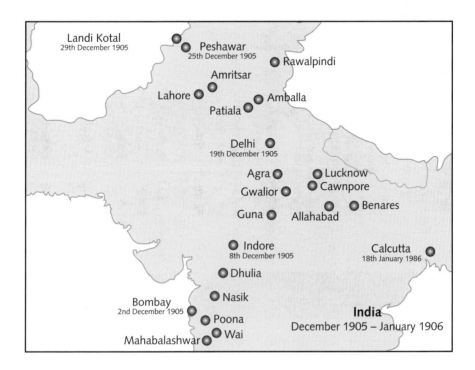

They drove from the pier to the new Taj Mahal Hotel. For Charles Thomas India was not a new experience but for the Gliddens it was their first glimpse of the country, and they were impressed by what they saw. A great mass of humanity filled the streets. In Glidden's own words, published in the *Boston Globe*, 7 January 1906:

> There was the dark-skinned Hindu coolie, naked but for a cloth about the loins, mingling with the rich white-gowned Parsi, wearing a small thimble shaped hat. Decked with a green turban was the follower of Mahomet, tall and erect. Then the odd looking men from Afghanistan and Baluchistan, the Bengali, Sikh, Maratha and Rajput, each in native costume, wending their way among Christians wearing the summer dress of Europe and America.

Of all this multifarious throng it was the Parsis that most interested Glidden. Their monotheistic beliefs, which rejected asceticism, instead emphasising moral choice and active participation in society, were more in accord with his Methodism than any other eastern religion. Parsis also appealed to his commercial instincts, tending to be enterprising and entrepreneurial. Many of them were successful businessmen. For these reasons he sought introduction and was invited to a Parsi wedding.

It was one of only two occasions when Glidden included his wife's comments in a letter intended for publication in the *Boston Globe*. He may have been forced into doing so because she was allowed access to parts of the ceremony from which men were excluded. These are her words as he reported them:

> As I entered the hall of ceremony, I found seated a large number of Parsee ladies, handsomely costumed and ornamented with jewels. The gentlemen in white suits were outside the main building. Musicians were playing in the illuminated garden. The ceremony in the Persian language being one hour in length the bride and bridegroom remain seated. No widows were with the company; they watched the proceedings from an anteroom. Elderly women were chanting a wedding blessing. The bride carried in her hand a coconut. The groom's sister, acting for his mother, who was a widow, sprinkled the bride's head with perfumes, placed a garland of flowers around her neck and presented her a tray of beautiful gifts, dresses and money.
>
> The bridegroom appeared dressed in white, carrying a cashmere shawl on his left arm. Two eggs were broken on the steps and a sheet was held between the bridal pair, so that they could not see each other. Under the sheet they grasped right hands. The high priest tied their wrists together by white cord and wound many yards of it about the chairs reciting the admonition for them to be faithful to each other. The sheet was withdrawn signifying no separation. The groom made the promise three times and the priests then chanted blessings, and threw

rice over the couple. Each put their right hands into a bowl of hot water, the bride dropping in five rupees as a thank offering. Her feet were then bathed in milk by a sister and upon the bridegroom making a contribution, his feet were also given the same treatment. Paternal blessings followed. Friends then approached, presenting the bride envelopes containing money. The bridal couple retired to the sacred fire, then followed refreshments.

At the Towers of Silence they were permitted to witness a Parsi funeral. The body was followed by mourners reciting prayers and the procession wended its way up the long hill. Next came a man leading a white dog, the emblem of faithfulness. The procession was completed by white-robed priests who led relatives and friends linked together with white handkerchiefs.

On the summit of the towers flocks of vultures waited. While the service was in progress bearers placed the naked body on an iron platform. It took less than two hours for the vultures to tear every scrap of flesh from the bones which were then allowed to whiten in the sun before being placed in a large well to dissolve and run into the sea, so making rich and poor alike, equal in death.

A few days were spent motoring around Bombay, through narrow lanes crowded with all manner of traffic. On the road to the Walkeshwar temples they drove by orange-robed beggars who wandered from one shrine to another throughout India. At the temples they saw naked, ash-smeared fakirs with long, filthy hair coiled upon their heads.

Glidden was impressed by the terminus of the Great Indian Peninsular Railway, which claimed to be the finest in the world. Their hotel, the new Taj Mahal, was the best in Asia and would have been a credit to any metropolitan city.

The presence of plague was a cause of concern and they occasionally passed a victim being taken to the hospital or crematorium. They were told a sad tale of an American family living in Bombay whose 11-year-old daughter had been playing with a pet dog when it caught and killed a rat. That night the little girl came down with the plague and died within twenty-four hours. The mother also fell prey to the disease and remained for three weeks in a critical condition, but eventually recovered.

They enjoyed a visit to the horse market. The finest Arabian horses were on offer from dealers who served lunch to prospective buyers. In another market they were offered a tiger cub for the price of a farthing's worth of curry powder.

During their stay in Bombay they saw many interesting native ceremonies, among them a reception for a celebrated maharajah from the Oudh district to the north. He was a devout Muslim and had just returned from a pilgrimage to Mecca. The maharaja travelled in regal style, together with his servants, occupying one half of a steamer. He was adorned with many valuable jewels and sat in a chair of solid gold.

The Gliddens were presented to the maharajah in an upper room of a Parsi mansion and enjoyed a brief conversation by means of an interpreter. There was a feast to celebrate the end of Ramadan and the next day a performance by nautch dancing girls.

One Sunday they attended the Bowen Methodist Memorial church. Dr Johnson of New York preached while the congregation was kept cool by huge punkahs operated by Indian servants pulling long ropes.

Glidden was guest of honour at a banquet given by the Motor Union of Western India. In conversation, the Deputy Commissioner of Police told Glidden that:

> We have just passed through a period of great anxiety during the visit of the Prince and Princess of Wales, but all went off well. There is a very rigid line between each caste of Hindu, Muslim and Sikh and other races, and I doubt if it can ever be broken down. It is much stronger than the prejudice against the black race in your south. A slight variance between two of a different caste or religion spreads into a struggle in which several thousand may be engaged, and it is difficult to end the disturbance without bloodshed.

Hindu nationalists were mounting a campaign encouraging the native population to boycott British manufacturers but at this stage without any great success.

Arrangements were completed for the long drive to Calcutta (now Kolkata). They were issued driving certificates and an Indian licence plate. The Bombay Motor Company arranged for supplies of petrol, oil and spare parts to be sent ahead to nine major stopping places between Bombay and the Afghan frontier; another six supply depots were set up between Delhi and Calcutta. Bullocks and native labour were arranged to assist in fording rivers and permission was obtained to cross five large rivers on railway bridges. Where there were no hotels, keepers of dak (rest) bungalows were notified to have food and accommodation ready.

Two native servants were hired, one to go in advance with bedding, and the other to ride on the car as an interpreter. Many people applied for these positions, presenting letters of reference, one of which said that the bearer was 'fairly honest'.

After his first ride in the Napier, the Parsi interpreter chosen declared that he wanted to go to America to become a chauffeur. Asked, 'Suppose you should die in America? There are no vultures there to eat your flesh.' He replied, 'If I die in a Christian country I will receive a Christian burial.'

Although the car had been released by customs it took some days for all the paperwork to be completed. Glidden considered these difficulties to be exceeded only by those encountered in the United States. It was his only home-like experience of the Indian tour.

At 6 a.m. on Saturday 2 December 1905, they commenced their tour with a short journey south onto the Deccan plateau.

Motoring along Queens Road, they passed the burning ghats and stopped to witness the ceremonies. The air was filled with the scent of burning sandalwood as Hindu corpses were cremated. All the while mourners chanted, accompanied by the ringing of bells and the clashing of cymbals. Later they passed fakirs preparing themselves for a pilgrimage to the Ganges who sat before burning embers doing penance, while around them boys beat drums.

Passing through the narrow streets, they reached the Sion Causeway which connected Bombay to the mainland. A few miles further on, the route turned south on the Madras road. The village streets they passed through were filled with people going to and fro with merchandise and farm products, while two-wheeled tongas carried passengers. Occasionally teams of wagon bullocks would rush, out of control, to the side of the road, spilling the load they were drawing. At one village, set amongst coconut groves, a blindfolded bullock was walking round a treadmill, raising water from a pond into an irrigation ditch.

Natives smiled and cheered as the motor car swept by or crowded around when it halted while priests and native officials saluted them with a grand salaam, bending and reaching to the earth with their right hands, then striking their foreheads two or three times which symbolised the placing of their heads beneath the motorists' feet.

Glidden recorded that the roads were good and the climb of 2,600ft over the Western Ghats was on an excellent, well-protected highway. The view from the summit, over broken volcanic land to the sea, reminded him of the Grand Canyon.

Their first night's stop was outside Poona, in the Deccan, where they were met by Aga Shah Rooks Shah, a cousin of the Aga Khan, and descendant of the Prophet Mohammed. Commenting on a photograph taken of their arrival in Poona, *The Autocar* said, 'it would seem that as the tour lengthens Thomas becomes more travel stained, Mr Glidden stouter and Mrs Glidden more handsome; only the car remains the same.'

They visited the temple of the Goddess Pārbati, where a priest told them:

I was created by God a Brahman and why should I not remain one? To be converted to Christianity would be against God's will. If he had wished me to be a Christian he would have created me as such. God, who created us, will preserve and destroy. God is everywhere. We are equal to him. Your God is my God. You reach him through Christ, the Parsis through created things such as earth, fire and water, Buddhists through Buddha, Mohammedans through their prophet. There is only one God and we reach him through the trinity of Brahma, Vishnu and Shiva. The idols are symbols and our people, until they are educated must reach the Creator through them. The time will come when the idols will be dispensed with but not until you give up the cross symbolic of your Christ.

Visiting the cave temple of Kali, a fakir mistook the Napier for the sacred carriage of juggernaut and, gripped by religious frenzy, attempted to throw himself beneath the car's wheels. He was held back by more sensible companions who told him that Glidden was a 'White Maharajah' whereupon he held out his hand, expecting a gift of alms.

On 3 December they continued south over three mountain passes, on an excellent road, to the hill station of Mahabaleshwar, situated on a tableland at an altitude of 4,600ft. Here they encountered a woman riding on the back of a donkey and asked if they might take her photograph. Looking alarmed she moved away, whilst their interpreter explained her behaviour saying, 'Don't touch her, for she is carrying food, and if touched by a Christian will not eat it.' However, when offered a few coins, she did pose for a photograph as did a little Hindu boy who knelt in prayer before a statue of the Lord Shiva.

From Mahabaleshwar they passed through the sacred village of Wai where many picturesque temples dedicated to the Hindu gods stood on the banks of the River Krishna.

From Wai they drove back to Bombay, where Glidden inspected a government research laboratory used for the preparation of plague vaccine. The bacteria was grown in vats, killed and then refined.

The same laboratory also produced snake bite serum. They watched as an Indian assistant caught a large cobra by the neck and squeezed until it opened its mouth. The creature's fangs were then pushed through a rubber membrane stretched over a glass vessel and the venom forced out.

# 12

# INDIA: NORTH-WEST FRONTIER

The long drive to Afghanistan started half an hour before sunrise on 6 December. Their route was north-east to Gwalior and Agra, then north-west through Delhi. This avoided having to cross the famine-stricken area of Rajasthan. After Delhi they intended to follow the Grand Trunk Road through Lahore, Rawalpindi and Peshawar to the Khyber Pass.

At Kalyan the small ferry was barely large enough for the car and it took an hour to load. Fifty miles further north they entered jungle. Occasional leopards, frightened by the car, ran across the road and cobras basked in the sun. They passed flocks of goats and sheep, also donkeys laden with teak and bamboo.

Boarding the ferry at Kalyan. (Author's collection)

They stopped for the night in a government rest-house at Nasik, 130 miles from Bombay. Its Khansame (keeper) provided a meal of chicken, eggs and mutton. That night they slept uneasily, with fire-arms close at hand, because thieves were rumoured to be in the district.

The following day disaster almost struck when, whilst fording a river, they sank in quicksand. Luckily, a crowd of villagers managed to pull them out and a grateful Glidden gave them thirty-three annas.

One hundred and seven miles further on they came to Dhulia, where they saw a chain-gang working on the streets. They also saw women grinding corn and children winding yarn into a long skein by walking a bobbin round sticks stuck in the ground.

The party's rest that night was more secure because they paid 66 cents as protection money to the head of the local thieves, the Chowkidar, who set one of his gang to stand guard with a drawn sabre.

On the third day of the drive they continued north to Indore. It was a rough road through jungle and Glidden described the people they passed as 'bronzed and dark skinned, with black, matted, tangled hair'. The car caused great excitement and drivers of bullock carts gave way with elaborate salaams.

At the Tapti River they met their first serious obstacle; it was 100 yards wide, 40 inches deep and fast flowing. There was no ferry or bridge and so twelve bullocks and a crowd of villagers were needed to get them across. Once on the other side Glidden lined everyone up and gave out rewards. Villagers received two annas each and the bullock drivers a rupee – then the village constable and its overseer came forward also demanding a rupee each.

Fording the Tapti River. (Author's collection / *Boston Sunday Globe*)

Beyond the Nerbudda River, crossed by a ferry, they met a camel caravan carrying goods from Afghanistan and Kashmir. Later they met Sikhs whose caravan was escorted by armed guards because it was laden with gold and silver. Next came a herd of wild camels which ran ahead of the car and attacked Charles Thomas when he tried to head them off.

Reaching Indore, Major Roberts, an army surgeon and acquaintance of Glidden's, gave them accommodation in his spacious bungalow within the British cantonments. Indore, situated as it was on the plateau of Central India, was ideal for the cultivation of opium poppies. In a letter to the *Boston Globe*, Glidden made no comment other than to put the annual value of opium exports to China at $35 million.

The nominal ruler of the province was a 17-year-old maharajah whose father had been deposed for attempting to poison the British political agent who actually controlled affairs. The maharajah was away at school so an introduction at the palace was not possible. However, the maharani was in residence. She lived in purdah, under the supervision of an English governess. Protocol meant that Mr Glidden was prevented from meeting her, but Mrs Glidden took his place. This is her description of the occasion:

> The queen received me assisted by her husband's twin sister. The queen is olive in complexion, tiny and frail looking but interesting from the fact that she is a finer type than most of her caste. She wore a white sari with gold border and pearl jewels. She was even pretty as she offered her tiny hand and bade me welcome in very good English. She has been studying five months. Her progress m writing and needle work which she was proud to exhibit was a great surprise. Our conversation was on education and American and English customs. To my statements she gave close attention. In bidding me goodbye she said I am very glad to see you, come again and she wished me a pleasant journey.

Further north they entered a native state ruled by a maharajah who sent his officers to clear the road for them and ordered a deputy commissioner to receive them on his behalf. Glidden reported that the day's run was made on a good but very dusty road and that the road skirted a district suffering a drought, only 10 inches of rain having fallen that year rather than the usual fifty-six. They therefore passed thousands of people, together with their flocks, who were on the move in an effort to escape the famine.

On 11 December 1905 they arrived in Gwalior, where the Maharajah Madhow Rao Scindia sent a letter of welcome. They were escorted to his palace, which was situated in several hundred acres of parkland, and given rooms and servants.

The maharajah, already a motoring enthusiast, was well informed about Glidden's journeys and enjoyed a ride in the Napier. Acting as his own chauffeur, he drove them to review troops who were being drilled for a parade in honour of the Prince and Princess of Wales who were about to make a state visit. Gwalior's native cavalry passed the reviewing stand, followed by six massive elephants drawing heavy guns and lifting their trunks in salute.

The Hindu religious laws prevented the maharajah from dining with them so they ate separately. Immediately after the meal, however, the men met the maharajah in the drawing room while Mrs Glidden was shown to the apartments of the maharani.

From Gwalior they drove to Agra, where they stayed a few days to see the sights and attend the festivities in honour of the Prince and Princess of Wales. The Gliddens received an invitation to the royal reception, which was a brilliant affair with British officers in full dress uniform whilst the maharajahs and princes wore all their jewelled finery.

On Tuesday 19 December they resumed the drive north to Delhi, passing through Aligarh where they joined the Grand Trunk Road, a magnificent highway extending 1,500 miles from the Afghan frontier town of Peshawar to Calcutta and called by Kipling the 'River of Life' because of the numbers and varieties of people and traffic it carried.

The Muslim guide and interpreter employed as Glidden and Charles entered the Islamic provinces of north-west India. (Author's collection)

They spoke with a Brahman who had been educated by Christian missionaries. He said, 'Our people talk much; but no European will ever know our true thoughts. The missionaries are doing good work in the way of educating and making some converts to Christianity: but it will take 10,000 years to Christianise India; Hinduism is an old religion and it serves us well.'

They began to see significant signs of famine on their drive. Glidden likened the land to the deserts of Arizona. Rain had not fallen for four months and was not expected for another five. All over the country, wells were running dry and the irrigation channels were empty. There were hosts of people on the move with barely enough flesh to cover their bones. Some lay dying by the wayside. Many were already dead. A tremendous irrigation canal was being built to relieve the disaster, but it was a long way from the snows of the Himalayas to the arid plains.

After Delhi they left the Hindu provinces and entered those where Islam predominated. They were joined by a new, Muslim, guide who said to them: 'You say Jesus, son of God: we say Jesus, prophet of God, and Mohammed, prophet of God.' Their routine continued much as before: Every day they drove about 150 miles; 100 before lunch, taken at noon, and the remainder before 4 p.m. They lunched by the roadside, enjoying watching all manner of people passing by.

At Ambala a branch road turned north to Simla, the summer capital of India but, because of snow in the ravines, they were unable to reach this most important of hill stations.

Reaching the Punjab, they passed through Sirhind, Ludhiana and Jullundur, after which the River Sutlej barred their progress. Luckily it was low so that, with the aid of a bullock team, they were able to cross.

Beyond Lahore there was danger from religious fanatics; travelling after dark was dangerous and the authorities could not guarantee their safety. In this region life was of very little value. Tribesmen carried on blood feuds for generations. Afridis, Afghans and Swats crowded the bazaars and a Mullah would often persuade one of these faithful that the death of a Christian would be rewarded with immediate entry into paradise. The punishment for such a murder if caught was to be hanged, the body then wrapped in a pig skin and burned – the Muslim equivalent of complete physical and spiritual extinction.

To assist the motorists through this troubled region, Major John Hill of the 15th Sikhs joined the Napier and remained with them until they had crossed the most dangerous parts of the area.

They reached Rawalpindi on Christmas Eve and 62 miles further west they crossed the Indus on a combined rail and road bridge. At Nowshera, 17 miles further on, they reached the Kabul River which rose in Afghanistan. They crossed it by way of a pontoon bridge and continued northward for 50 miles, on a military road, to the frontier of Swat.

The frontier fort at Malakand. (Author's collection)

An invitation had been sent to them by the assistant political officer of Malakand to visit its famous frontier fort, which they reached via a road that wound its way over a pass amidst superb scenery. Armed guards where everywhere and nearly every person carried a rifle or dagger. There was no punishment for murders committed more than 50ft from the main road.

Christmas Day found them in Peshawar, a place so dangerous that Europeans could not venture out after dark. Despite this, Glidden wrote to the British authorities asking for access to the Khyber Pass which was, as now, of extreme military and political significance. Russia's railways reached far into central Asia. Britain, wanting to keep Russia away from India, needed to maintain Afghanistan as a buffer state and so large numbers of British troops, under the command of Lord Kitchener, were being assembled on the North-west Frontier. If war did break out it was not certain who the Afghans would side with.

Considering the strategic sensitivity of the region, it is a mark of Glidden's influence that his letter brought this reply:

Peshawar Station.

Undersigned has the honour to inform you, in reply to your letter of the 13th inst. To the honourable chief commissioner that visitors are not allowed to proceed beyond Al Maaji, which is only thirty miles from Peshawar. They are only allowed to go there on Tuesdays and Fridays. Come to my office when you arrive in Peshawar and I will try and arrange for you to drive with the motor car through the Khyber Pass as far as Landi Kotal.

Major George O. Roos-Keppel.
Political officer of the Khyber.

Landi Kotal was a British fort 2 miles inside Afghanistan and to reach it Major Roos-Keppel, a fluent Pashto speaker responsible for keeping peace amongst the warlike tribes of the region, took significant precautions. Heavily armed men of the Khyber Rifles were positioned along the road with orders to guard every inch of the Napier's progress.

East meets west in the Khyber Pass. Major Roos-Keppel is leaning across in front of Mr Glidden. (Author's collection)

On 29 December, a cool crisp morning, they left Peshawar to drive through the pass. A caravan of 500 camels, as well as hundreds of donkeys and bullocks, had already started ahead of them and, 13 miles away at Landi Kotal, an even larger caravan, loaded with merchandise from central Asia, had started towards India.

The road was smooth with a rising grade to the fort at Jamrud, where Glidden's party crossed into Afghan territory. The way now became steep and narrow. On either side were tribal villages; built of mud brick, they appeared more like small forts complete with curtain walls, a single entrance and sentry towers. Men, armed with knives and rifles, often lounged at their gates waiting for an opportunity to rob the unwary or sometimes to settle a blood feud with an enemy.

Eleven miles beyond the next British fort, at Al Masjid, they overtook the Indian caravan before meeting the Afghan caravan in the territory of the troublesome Bakkukhel tribe who, the night before, had raided a rival village, killing several people.

It was here that the Napier suffered a puncture. Many armed Afghans gathered to watch the repairs. Some of them, in return for a small reward, helped pump up

The Afghan caravan. (Author's collection)

Landi Kotal. (Author's collection)

the tyre but Glidden believed that only the presence of the Khyber Rifles kept him and his party safe.

At Landi Kotal the commanding officer told them the Napier was only the third motor vehicle to reach that point. Of the other two, one was driven by a Mr Phipps of Pittsburgh, Pennsylvania; the other was sent through to Kabul, probably as a diplomatic gift for the Amir of Afghanistan.

From the Khyber Pass they returned along the Grand Trunk Road, crossing the Indus on the Attock Bridge. Every land-born invasion of India had passed that way since the time of Alexander the Great. The fort was built by Akbar in 1583 and the extensive views reached as far as the snows of the Hindu Kush.

# 13

# India: Grand Trunk Road

Passing through Lahore and Amritsar, they reached the Sikh state of Patiala, where they became guests of His Highness the Maharajah Bopindra Singh who accommodated them in a guesthouse situated in the Moti Bagh, the Pearl Garden, an area luxuriantly planted with flowers, shrubs and trees of many varieties. There they were visited by the British assistant political agent and by the general commanding the Maharajah's native army who invited them to watch a dress parade, which included artillery drawn by elephants and a large camel corps.

Riding the state elephants of Patiala. (Author's collection)

The following day two state elephants, decked in cloth of red and gold, and bearing howdahs of gold and silver, appeared in the garden. The mahouts made the elephants kneel so that Glidden's party could mount, after which they rode to the old palace, where they saw the crown jewels of Patiala.

Indian businessmen called on them, curious to know about America. Many expressed their wish to visit a land where freedom ruled. According to Glidden one Muslim said:

We are not receiving the education we would like. It is education that opens the eyes of the idols and the people. We are grateful to America for its charity in educating our children regardless of the religion they may follow after leaving the schools. I was educated in a missionary school. The time must come when India will have government by the people. Now it is practically all military rule, especially in the Northern provinces. England is afraid to educate us for fear of our declaring independence. We would be satisfied to govern ourselves like the Canadians. One thing, the English have made it possible for us to go about India. Previous to their coming here we could not leave our villages. England certainly guarantees the peace of India, but we Mohammedans are not satisfied.

This was a view apparently shared in part by a British officer, who said, 'We fear the Mohammedans will give us trouble and the fiftieth anniversary of the Mutiny in 1907 may witness disturbing things in the country. The only thing that will prevent trouble is the rigid caste and the failure to unite the native tribes.'

Glidden and his party were invited to the home of a Sikh, which Glidden described as a rather dingy house of stone and mortar. Narrow stairs led to the roof which was used as a reception room. Ladies, dressed in pantaloons and blouses, offered them cardamom seeds and wine, which the Gliddens, as good Methodists, declined.

Glidden thought the Sikhs a very promising sect, ready to adopt modern ideas. He stated that they made good soldiers and approved of the fact that their women were not veiled. He considered that India would remain in darkness until its women were educated and free to go unveiled.

On Sunday, 7 January 1906 they arrived back at Agra, where they arranged the transfer of heavy baggage to Calcutta and the shipment of gasoline to supply depots.

A long drive took them across the United Provinces, but 15 miles east of Etawa the road became impassable so they followed a canal bank for 60 miles until they reached Cawnpore. The following day they crossed the Ganges and drove north to visit Lucknow.

Allahabad, situated at the junction of the holy rivers Jumna and Ganges, was packed with people, all there for the great Hindu festival of Magh Mele. The

The scene at a Hindu festival. (Author's collection)

crowd was estimated at 2 million. Cholera and smallpox were rife. It was expected that during the sixty-day festival there would be 2,000 deaths as well as 400 births.

Pilgrims had come from all over India, some crawling on hands and knees only to fall dead from exhaustion as they arrived. Others bore the ashes of dead relatives to be scattered on the waters of the sacred rivers.

There were beggars innumerable. Glidden considered the thousands of fakirs to be a ghastly sight of self-inflicted depravity. Some had held their hands above their heads until the arms had become rigid, making it impossible to lower them.

Driving became difficult because the roads were crowded with people making their way to the great festival. Absorbed in the holy purpose of their journey, they did not respond to the sound of the car's horn.

Under the shade of a sacred peepul tree, Glidden's party talked with a man, his wife and daughter, whose feet were sore and swollen from walking.

'Where are you going?'

'To Prahag (Allahabad) the festival.'

'How far have you travelled?'

'1,200 miles.'

'How many miles a day?'

'About twenty.'

'Where do you sleep nights?'

'On the ground.'

'What do you eat?'

'Whatever God gives us.'

'What does he give you?'

'Bread.'

They interviewed a fakir, whose body was smeared with grease and ash, learning that he travelled continually across India and had recently walked 1,040 miles from the Punjab.

'Why don't you work like other people?'

'Why should I work? I pray all day long for the people.'

'Where do you get food?'

Pointing upward, he said, 'From the sky.'

The high day of the Magh Mel was celebrated by wealthy Hindus, mounted on elephants and camels, distributing alms to the people, after which the crowds bathed in the Ganges. According to Hindu belief, the moment the water touched their body sin was washed away and they became ritually pure.

On 16 January the group stayed in Benares as guests of the Rev. Rockwell Clancy, treasurer of the Methodist Episcopal Church Missions for Southern Asia. After sunset they witnessed the offering of fire to the sacred river. Positioned in a

Nepalese pilgrims on their way to the Ganges. (Author's collection)

boat opposite the main temple, they heard the clanging of bells summoning the people to the ceremony. In memory of the dead, earthenware lamps were lit and floated away on small rafts.

A priest swung a burning torch back and forth as many in the crowd put their hands into the flame and touched their own foreheads, signifying purification. The priest then carried the torch to the river bank and emptied its contents into the water.

The following day, a Sunday, Glidden took great satisfaction in attending a service at the Mission church, where Indian boys and girls sang hymns in Hindi. He very much approved of the work done by missionaries, not only for spreading Christianity but also for educating the children. After the service the Gliddens joined a procession which passed through both Hindu and Islamic districts of the city without any reaction from the populous, even though the Christian women went unveiled.

Off the Grand Trunk Road to the north they visited the Buddhist shrine of Buddha Gaya. The temple dated to 543 BC and marked the place where Buddha was believed to have received the enlightenment.

The drive down the entire length of the Grand Trunk Road from Peshawar to Calcutta was completed on 18 January 1906. Mr and Mrs Glidden then went by rail to Darjeeling whilst Charles Thomas gave the Napier a service, which it needed after the 4,405-mile drive. The work was carried out in the railway workshops. The engine was thoroughly overhauled and the lubricating oil changed.

# 14

# THE ROAD TO MANDALAY

On Friday 25 January the car was loaded on the British India Steamship Company's new mail boat, SS *Bangala*, bound for Rangoon, the capital of Burma. The 785-mile voyage across the Bay of Bengal was pleasant and took seventy-four hours, including a twenty-four-hour wait for mail and tide.

There were many contrasts between the India they had left and the Burma they were entering. After the Himalayas, where the thermometer averaged 40°F

Visiting a Burmese temple. (Author's collection)

with a heavy frost each night, Mr and Mrs Glidden found the climate delightful. The landscape varied from dry and parched to humid jungle. There was no caste system nor any veiled women. Burmese woman were free to conduct business and go about at will, though it was disconcerting to see people of all ages, even young children, smoking cheroots. It was not an unusual sight to see a baby at its mother's breast take a whiff from the large cigar she was smoking, a cigar 8 inches long and three in circumference. Everywhere they went they were met with courtesy and kindness.

Buddhist temples and pagodas abounded, tended by monks dressed in saffron yellow robes. The greatest pagoda in the world, the Shwe Dagon, was entirely covered in gold leaf and attracted worshippers from all over the east. Despite his Methodist opinions, Glidden was strangely impressed by the sight of a beautiful young Burmese girl kneeling before a statue of the Buddha, with head bowed and eyes closed, to say a prayer she had probably learned from her mother. On completing the prayer she touched her head three times to the flagstones then placed an offering of flowers upon the marble image.

At the Steele Brothers' timber mill they saw elephants at work piling teak logs. The animals showed much intelligence and strength as they raised 1-ton logs high in the air or rolled them into position with their trunks and tusks. The elephants were very careful not to break a tusk, and often placed their trunk between a tusk and a particularly heavy timber.

Modern machinery was by then replacing elephants in the saw mills but in the forests they remained the only means of moving teak logs from the felling sites to the rivers along which they were floated down to the mills. Whenever there was a log jam an experienced team of elephant and rider was needed to remove the key log and start the timber on its way again.

Rangoon and its suburbs were well laid out with macadamised roads. The soil was red and very dusty and the streets were full of people from a variety of nationalities.

They drove 55 miles from Rangoon to Pegu to see the famous statue of the reclining Buddha. Built of bricks and mortar, the statue was 180ft long and 16ft high at the shoulder. The face had a pleasant smile and the sole of one foot was inlaid with coloured glass. It was discovered in 1881, buried in the jungle, and a building of brick and steel was being erected to protect it.

The drive back to Rangoon was made through clouds of dust thrown up by many bullock carts with handsomely decorated yokes. Their Burmese owners, along with neatly dressed families that might number as many as ten or fifteen, were taking a late afternoon drive, after which they would call on friends, have a smoke and eat sweetmeats.

A continuous tour was not possible in Burma because there were only 600 miles of made-up road, consisting of many widely separated and disconnected sections. His Excellency, the Lieutenant Governor, supplied them with maps of existing roads and gasoline was purchased in at the price of 28 cents a gallon. By using the railway and river steamers they managed to travel some of the more accessible routes.

There were problems arranging for the motor car to be taken by rail on the 356-mile journey to Mandalay because Burmese railroad officials had not yet learned that gasoline could be carried on their trains. The Indian railways had been doing so for more than a year. The Burmese officials finally allowed 13 gallons to be taken on the car.

Supervised by Charles Thomas, thirty native labourers loaded the car onto a mixed passenger/goods train which departed at 6.30 a.m. on Sunday 4 February and arrived at noon the following day. Mr and Mrs Glidden travelled by a much faster mail train.

The journey took them through jungle and passed great rice paddies whose contented owners sat by the track smoking cheroots. Their wives did most of the actual work besides managing household affairs, buying the daily supplies and taking care of the family. There was hardly a single house in a village that did not have something for sale, such as dried fish, betel nuts, cardamoms, coconuts or fabrics woven on hand looms by the young girls. When the rice was safely harvested and sold there would be a great celebration with a feast and charitable donations to the poor.

The houses were built of bamboo and stood on poles 7 or 8ft high but were limited to one floor only because no Burmese would allow anyone to walk overhead. The homes of wealthier folk were built of teak with an occasional tiled roof instead of the more usual thatch. Preparation and cooking of food was done in open air courtyards where white ants took possession of everything.

There were many bullock carts, each of which had a bunch of bananas attached to the tip of the pole, carried there to appease capricious spirits known as 'Nats'. Belief in 'Nats' was widespread. Every person was supposed to have their own 'Nat' and every house its guardian 'Nat' to whom offerings would be made. No one thought of eating without first holding his plate high in the air and offering a prayer to the village 'Nat'.

The Gliddens arrived at their Mandalay hotel soon after sunrise and found no one awake to receive them or show the way to their room. Servants were still sleeping outside their employers' rooms but soon there were calls of 'Boy, bring some tea' or 'Is my bath ready?' followed by a stir and chatter among the servants and at the same time the crows set up their morning calls.

The Napier was safely unloaded from its railway wagon and the Gliddens were amused to see that a small fire extinguisher had been placed ready behind it. Had a fire started then the 32 gallons of gasoline in the tank would have made quick work of everything.

Within and around Mandalay there were 225 miles of very dusty roads made of hard-rolled sand. As well as Burmese, they saw a great many other peoples: Chins from the eastern mountains, Shans wearing immense straw hats, Kachins from the north, Chinese from Yunnan and a few Sikhs, Ghurkhas and Hindus from Madras. The city was policed by Sikhs from the Punjab who did all in their power to make driving on the busy roads pleasant.

The Gliddens needed to obtain local currency and the money changer was a young woman with a white powdered face who consented to pose for a photograph, but not with the large cigar she was smoking in her mouth. She said, 'my husband would object to a picture with the cigar shown.'

Hundreds of yellow-robed priests, with their black begging bowls, were calling at houses whose owners made contributions of food. The priests said nothing, not showing any gratitude for what was given them. The motorists watched one particular house and saw fifteen priests beg for alms. Each time the owner, a wealthy Burmese lady, gave rice, vegetables and copper coins. One of the begging priests agreed to stand before the camera, but his benefactor refused. The Gliddens followed the priest through the market place and watched as he received yet more donations, even seeming to choose the kind of vegetables he wanted. Everything was freely given, without a single word of complaint.

Glidden made an effort to reach the Northern Shan states, but only succeeded in getting as far as the summit of a mountain 23 miles to the east of Mandalay from where the frontier could be seen. Further progress was blocked by large boulders and deep ruts.

The Burmese money changer. (Author's collection)

An elephant working in the teak mills. (Author's collection)

Some peculiar characters were met on the road, people from not only the Shan states but from Yunnan, an adjoining province of China, all tramping along loaded with produce and merchandise for the Mandalay bazaar. They wore wide conical hats, 30 inches in diameter. The motor car completely bewildered them; some even dropped their burdens and ran into the jungle. The camera scared them nearly as much, but the interpreter, a Kachin from the upper Irrawaddy, forcibly lined up a half dozen men and women for a photograph. After all was over, and their fear proved groundless, broad grins appeared on their faces and some of the bolder ones jeered at the timid.

They drove 6 miles south of Mandalay to Amarapura, the old capital of Upper Burmah, which was founded by King Bodopaya in 1782. This was a place of extensive ruins, which had now become a busy silk manufacturing district. Nearly every house had a number of hand looms in operation, all worked by young women.

The return to Rangoon was by river steamer down the Irrawaddy, a monotonous ride to Prome, 400 miles in three days, followed by 161 miles of railroad which took twelve hours. The captain of the river steamer did all in his power to make the voyage pleasant. The boat anchored at night and stopped at a number of places, including Pagan, but the Gliddens were disappointed that no time was allowed to visit the pagodas or the principal ruins.

# 15

# CEYLON

Under the supervision of Charles Thomas, the motor car was shipped directly from Rangoon to Ceylon (now Sri Lanka), a voyage of five days, on the steamer *Cheshire*. Meanwhile, Mr and Mrs Glidden returned to Calcutta aboard the *Bangala* with the intention of touring southern India by rail.

Glidden found this journey fatiguing, complaining that the overnight compartments of Indian trains were much inferior to those of their American

Passing through a village in Ceylon. (Author's collection)

equivalents. Before arrival in Madras (now Chennai) they were medically examined because, having travelled from the infected area of Calcutta, they needed a plague passport certifying them free of the disease.

In Tanjore (now Thanjavur) they witnessed Hindu fakirs practising extreme forms of asceticism. One hung by his heels above a small fire while another was buried to the neck in sand. Indeed, several European and American residents of the area had become followers of the fakirs. Glidden's strict religiosity and own brand of morals meant that he did not entirely approve of this.

On Monday 14 February they boarded a small British India steamer at Tuticorin, at the extreme southern end of India, for an overnight passage across the Gulf of Mannar to Colombo, where they presented their plague passports. Despite this, they each had to undergo a medical examination and were obliged to report daily to a government physician throughout the following week.

The motor car was safely transferred from the steamer to landing stage by means of a large flat-bottomed boat. The customs officers demanded payment of 5 per cent of its value as a deposit, which they promised to return on departure.

They drove from the docks through the broad city thoroughfare to their hotel. As in all Asian cities the entire road, as well as the pavement, were crowded with pedestrians. As they left the docks they were besieged by touts for various trade establishments offering cards and urging them to call at their places of business. The touts ran after them through the streets until they became exhausted, after which others rushed out of doorways to continue the pursuit. At the hotel almost the entire entrance terrace was taken up with merchants whose wares covered all available space, making it far more difficult to reach the reception desk than passing the crowd of cabmen at New York's Grand Central station. The words 'Epah Pallin', meaning 'I don't want anything, get out', were partially effective, if spoken with enough force.

From Colombo, on Ceylon's west coast, Glidden planned to reach the island's most eastern, northern and southern points. Before setting out he ensured that his arrangements for petrol depots across the island had been put in place and that an extra case of tyres had arrived from London. An hour after their arrival at the hotel all was in readiness for a drive to Kandy, high in the island's interior.

They began the journey on 21 February. The sky was cloudless and they first drove through crowded streets, then passed cinnamon gardens before crossing over the Kelangi Ganga River on the Victoria bridge and out among coconut plantations and paddy fields. The thermometer registered 90°F but, overhead, dense foliage shut out the rays of the sun. The road took them past native villages of which Glidden approved, describing them as being neat and thrifty.

Later they stopped to allow a funeral procession of a Buddhist nun to pass by. At the head of the line came dancers and buffoons performing to the sound of eastern music. Next came bullock carts carrying offerings for the priests, followed by the body, borne on a bamboo frame. The mourners talked and smiled, with no sign of grief. Thousands were present at the cremation, which Glidden thought looked to be more of a festival than a funeral.

Another 45 miles through plantation and jungle brought them to Kegalla, after which began the climb to Kandy, situated 1,700ft above sea level. Here they visited the temple containing a tooth thought to have been the Buddha's. The shrine housing the tooth was in the form of a lotus flower made of gold.

The following morning they left Kandy and drove over the Kotmalie Pass to Newera Eliya, then Badulla and on to Lunagalla, where they stopped for the night. The road was narrow and winding, climbing to a height of 6,200ft followed by a dangerous descent needing great care. At these altitudes the early morning temperature was only 50°F and they found the cool air delightful. The mountain

Repairing a puncture somewhere in Ceylon. (Author's collection)

sides were covered with plantations where women were at work picking tea leaves. There were also cinchona trees from which quinine was made, and also orange and lemon trees.

Continuing the drive on the 23rd, the motor car ascended the steepest grades on the island amid coffee plantations and some of the best mountain scenery yet encountered, then in a distance of 20 miles they descended 4,000ft to sea level and passed through groves of rubber trees, pineapples, poppy and coconut palm to Batticaloa on the east coast. Here unsatisfactory accommodation persuaded Glidden to return to Lunagalla, where the rest-house had provided excellent meals and service.

This change of plan required a two-hour drive in the dark. The Napier's powerful headlights bewildered the natives and frightened a variety of wild animals. First came a huge buffalo which ran ahead of the car for a mile before disappearing into the jungle. Several cheetahs and a tiger ran across the road, and they chased jackals for miles. Long-tailed monkeys scampered up into the trees, while clouds of flying insects dashed themselves against the headlights.

Leaving Lunagalla, they returned to Kandy over the Ramboda Pass, which, at 7,000ft, was the highest road in Ceylon and notorious for accidents. At the bottom of a cliff lay the remains of a car whose driver had lost control, but who had managed to save his life by leaping from the vehicle before it plunged over the edge. A horse-drawn carriage had not been so lucky, dropping 1,000ft into a ravine. All eight passengers, the driver and horses were killed.

The following Monday they drove north from Kandy to Dambulla, aiming to reach Jaffna in the far north. The road was excellent and the first 20 miles took them through wonderful scenery. To their right was the range of mountains known as the Knuckles, to the left the hills around Kandy, and before them the road zigzagged down for 2,000ft, passing through groves of cocoa, cardamoms and rubber, before reaching the lowland plains.

They soon learnt that bundles of straw lying in the road were, in reality, hazardous objects to be avoided, for they concealed large stones. Drivers of bullock cart were in the habit of building their cooking fires in the centre of the road. When finished they simply extinguished the fire and left the rocks used to contain it covered with straw.

From Dambulla the road ran north-east through dense jungle to Trincomalee. On the way they saw the occasional wild elephant as well as cheetahs, monkeys, buffalo and a huge python. They drove through an enormous cloud of butterflies, thousands of which were crushed under the wheels or caught in the radiator.

Turning aside, they followed a cart track to Sigiri where, on a rock rising 400ft from the plain, the patricide King Kasyapa had, in the fifth century, constructed a magnificent palace with rooms of great size all filled with marvellous sculpture.

King Kasyapa's rock at Segiri. (Author's collection)

The great port of Trincomalee was reached on the fourth day's drive, but since the signing of an Anglo-Japanese treaty its spacious harbour and military post were almost empty.

That evening Tamby, the Tamil rest-house keeper at Trincomalee, provided not only comfortable rooms but also a ten-course dinner. Disappointed by his guests' inability to eat everything, Tamby cheered up when Mr Glidden wrote a generous testimonial in the visitor's book he had kept during his forty-four years of service.

Half a day was spent motoring 60 miles from Trincomalee to Anuradhapura and again they saw a great deal of wildlife, including many jungle fowl and other birds all with colourful plumage. Eight miles from Anuradhapura they stopped to view the ancient ruins at Mihintale. A rocky hill was crowned with a 'dagoba', or Buddhist shrine, and covered with the remains of temples, monasteries and hermitages.

The group's interest was drawn to a nearby house which was surrounded by a crowd of people, six of whom, hideously daubed with paint, were dancing to the beating of drums and contorting themselves into strange postures. It was explained that a resident of the house was suffering from smallpox and a devil dance ceremony was being held to drive away the evil spirit that had brought the disease.

They stayed the night in a lonely rest-house deep in the jungle. The rest-house staff, working at very short notice, provided a delicious meal of chicken. The motorists couldn't help noticing that at the time of their arrival the chicken had still been scratching around the courtyard.

On Wednesday 28 February they drove on to Jaffna by way of Point Pedro, the most northerly point of Ceylon. Many of Jaffna's people were Christian and Glidden took note of the excellent educational work being done by American missionaries.

The tour of Ceylon was completed with a long drive from Jaffna, down the west coast, through the former Portuguese colony of Galle, to Dondra Head, the most southerly point of the island.

Returning to Colombo, the car was loaded aboard the Messageries Maritimes steamer *Armand Behic*, which sailed for Saigon (now Ho Chi Minh City) on 8 March.

# 16

# SAIGON

The voyage from Colombo to Saigon lasted a week, including time for a brief stop-over in Singapore. The *Armand Behic* carried thirty passengers, including many French officers returning to duty after their annual leave, and a dozen English tourists who were travelling around the world.

Glidden relished the food, especially the supply of fresh meat, made possible because the ship carried livestock, some of which were slaughtered every day. He

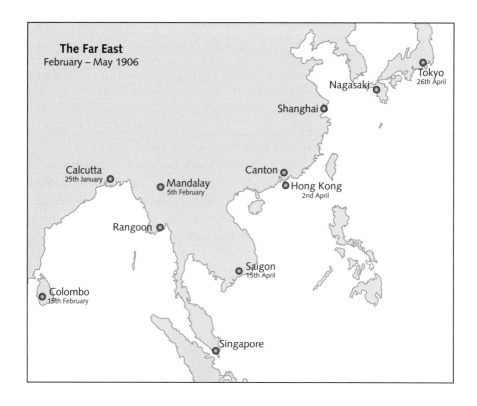

**The Far East**
February – May 1906

Tokyo
26th April

Nagasaki

Shanghai

Calcutta
25th January

Canton

Mandalay
5th February

Hong Kong
2nd April

Rangoon

Saigon
15th April

Colombo
15th February

Singapore

also approved of there being no spirits or champagne on board, though wine was served at lunch and dinner.

The passengers made their own entertainment with amateur theatricals performed in French. A partial attempt was made to include the Americans by providing them with written translations.

Glidden's religious principles did bring about one alteration to the ship's routine. It was usual, every Sunday, to hold a lottery in aid of a seaman's charity, but this was put back until the Monday.

They entered the estuary of the Saigon River on the afternoon of 15 March and headed 40 miles upriver, making fast to the pier at eight o'clock that evening. The winding channel was bordered by rice paddies with small villages built over the water on piles.

From the ship their first view of Saigon's many sizable buildings was impressive. Once alongside the quay two small bare-footed boys, wearing red jackets, short white trousers and red puttees, came aboard. They spoke both French and English and were there to conduct the Gliddens to the Hotel Continental where they took a suite of rooms. The hotel was Parisian in style but adapted to the Tropics with large open windows shaded by heavy blinds.

The Napier was found to have come to no harm during the voyage and the US Deputy Consul arranged for it to be landed, together with its crates of spare parts.

Early next morning a number of Chinese tailors came to the hotel seeking clients. Glidden placed an order, sending an existing suit with them from which they could take his measurements. His new suits were delivered that evening at a cost of $3 for a white business suit and $3.50 for a three-piece evening suit. The Chinese tailor made wide circular gestures to indicate that the extra 50 cents was for the additional material needed to cloth his rotund client.

Glidden had written in advance to the French Governor General to notify him of their impending arrival, but when they called he was absent in Tonquin. However, he had left instructions that they were to be provided with all necessary aid for their tour through the colony. As there was no suitable accommodation outside of the capital they were forced to end each day's drive by returning to the Hotel Continental.

Leaving Saigon, they drove south. The villages through which they passed were very poor. The people lived in huts constructed of nothing but bamboo and palm leaves. Despite this the vegetable gardens near Saigon and Cho Lon were well set out and productive.

As in Java, most loads were carried on the head or at either end of a long bamboo pole slung across one shoulder. This created a potential danger as, surprised by the car's headlights, a load bearer would turn to see what was coming and swing the pole across the road, blocking the way.

They crossed many small rivers on rickety bridges on their journey (Glidden estimated over 300) and at one point they came to one that had wholly collapsed. This forced a night-time diversion along rough cart tracks that ran through villages whose people crowded round the Napier, slowing its progress.

They were given special permission to visit the palace at Cho Lon, which consisted of a series of low Chinese-style buildings furnished with intricately carved furniture inlaid with pearl and ivory. The centrepiece of the palace was an altar dedicated to the Lord Buddha, before which offerings of fruit and flowers were laid.

On St Patrick's Day they drove 210 miles to Cape St Jacques, off which the Russian fleet had anchored en route to Japan and its defeat at the Battle of Tushima the previous May. As a telegrapher Glidden had a technical interest in Cape St Jacques, which was an important station for the submarine cables laid between Singapore and Hong Kong. The station's superintendent gave them lunch and showed them the instruments in his charge.

Glidden described some of the people in this area as 'primitives' who went naked with long, matted hair. They lived on fish and rice and were, in his opinion, harmless. Some were confused by the car, gathering round and wondering what type of monster it was. Others removed their hats, closed their umbrellas and bowed twice as the motorists went past, this being the manner in which Europeans were shown respect. However, it proved impossible to photograph the natives; the moment the camera appeared they fled.

A road, built northward by the French, stopped just short of the Cambodian border in an area inhabited by a tribe called the Mois, who had a violent reputation. French officials told Glidden that it was safe to meet with these people in daylight but at night they could be dangerous. Like others before them, the tribesmen proved very curious about the car and crowded around it but vanished at any sign of a camera.

There were man-eating tigers in the jungle, for which reason the tribal villages were built on tall piles and surrounded by bamboo palisades. As a precaution the Napier was given an armed escort. Whilst on the road the only other vehicles met with were mail-carrying bullock carts.

Their final drive in this region was to Tay Ninh, north-west of Saigon. Here the French were building a double line of concentric defences around the town. On the coast, Cape St Jacques was strongly fortified while roads and railways were being extended towards Thailand and Burma. France was evidently making ready to defend its colony, or to expand it should an opportunity occur. Glidden's observations persuaded him that the French were ideal colonisers, establishing schools and churches, and governing a large native population in an 'easy, quiet manner'.

The Gliddens sailed from Saigon on Friday 23 March aboard an elderly French coastal steamer bound for Haiphong and Hanoi. A week later the Napier, with Charles Thomas in charge, was loaded aboard a regular mail steamer and sent direct to Hong Kong to be joined by the Gliddens on 2 April, their small German-owned coaster having been delayed by rough seas in the Straits of Hainan.

# 17

# CHINA

After landing the Napier in Hong Kong it was discovered that careless loading in Saigon had resulted in scratched paint and bent fenders. However, they found the roads to be well suited to motoring, though very crowded with other forms of traffic. Coolies carried merchandise about, while wealthy Europeans rode around in rickshaws. On level ground there were electric trams and a funicular railway took passengers up the steep climb to the Peak.

The island's size limited opportunities for extended driving and so they left the car and took an overnight ferry up the Pearl River to Canton (now Guangzhou). Here they visited a 3,000-year-old Chinese city, with a population of 2½ million. On crowded moorings in the river a mass of junks and sampans housed half a million. Everywhere the Glidden party went they were stared at in wonder.

Street scene, Shanghai. (Author's collection)

Riding in a sedan chair, with a guide named Ah Kow, they explored the city, visiting temples, pagodas, coffin shops and execution grounds.

Returning to Hong Kong, they took the Napier across the harbour to Kowloon and the New Territories, where they visited several Chinese villages.

Forty miles by steamer took them to Macao; known as the Monte Carlo of the east, it was notorious for its many casinos. Avoiding these, Glidden visited a grotto dedicated to the Portuguese poet Camoens and the ancient Jesuit church of San Paulo.

On 10 April they sailed on the Occidental and Pacific mail steamer SS *Doric*, bound for Shanghai. The ship was crowded with passengers, many of them Filipino, as the ship's regular service included Manila as well as San Francisco, Yokohama and Shanghai. The north-east monsoon was blowing and the seas ran high, making the voyage cold and wet. They sailed through the Straits of Formosa and across the East China Sea, finally coming to anchor near Woosung, 18 miles from Shanghai. The harbour was full of vessels of many sorts, including passenger liners and tramp steamers as well as sailing junks. In Glidden's opinion their numbers indicated China's importance to world trade, but he was concerned that, in common with Rangoon, Columbo and Hong Kong, such a major port had no

No smiles for the camera in Shanghai. (Author's collection)

A Chinese wheelbarrow. (Author's collection)

quays where large ships could moor alongside. This meant going ashore aboard a launch while the Napier had to be offloaded on a lighter, which was both risky and expensive.

Touring Shanghai's historic walled city, they found its streets to be narrow and crowded. Sanitation was non-existent and the smell horrible beyond description. Shops opened directly onto the street with a work area and living quarters at the rear. Goods were carried about on barrows with one large wheel in the centre enabling one man to push a load weighing up to 800 pounds. Many of the rickshaws carried Chinese who were in an opium-induced stupor.

Through the open doors of a house they caught sight of a dead body surrounded by friends having a quiet smoke. On the threshold a woman wailed before a table on which were placed several plates of fruit for the deceased's journey into the unknown. Other people walked by, paying no attention to the ceremony.

The city gates were closed at sunset and it was very dangerous for foreigners to be out after dark so they decided to restrict further sight-seeing to the countryside or more modern areas.

Glidden was horrified to discover that the Chinese were buying Bibles not to read but to use the pages as wrapping for coins.

Many older women had bound feet, which was already an archaic custom possibly dating back as far as the T'ang dynasty. Although becoming less frequent, the practice was still inflicted upon some unfortunate young girls.

They spoke with a prosperous European silk merchant who said, 'The Chinese have many good business qualities. I make verbal contracts with them every year for hundreds of bales of raw silk. Not a word in writing passes between us and I never knew them to fail to live up to a contract, notwithstanding any unfavourable change to them in the market conditions.'

To guard against civil disorder, all the major powers had gunboats moored in the river. The last serious riot had taken place the previous December, resulting in twenty-five Chinese deaths. Rickshaws carrying foreigners were overturned

One of Shanghai's Sikh policemen. (Author's collection)

and European women dragged through the streets by their hair. The hotels and legations soon became crammed with people seeking protection.

Glidden discussed the 'problem' of China with Rev. Howard Agnew Johnson of New York who, on behalf of various missionary societies, was making a study of 'The Eastern Question'. Rev. Johnson identified a series of policies, enforced by the western powers, which China regarded as unjust. Among these were Britain's trade in opium, America's exclusion of Chinese immigrants, the use of military force to extort commercial and territorial concessions, resentment of missionary activity and the way foreigners generally behaved toward the Chinese. Since its victory over Russia, an increasingly confident Japan was urging the Chinese to boycott western, particularly American, goods.

Glidden's main excursion in China was a day's drive following the line of the Grand Canal, which had been constructed over many centuries between Hangchow and Tientsin. The return was made on the excellent roads of the French concession to the Bund, Shanghai's famous water front, followed by a circuit of the walled city which took them through several international concessions. Street names varied with the nationality of each concession: one minute they were on Broadway but just across a bridge the same road became the Rue Daumer.

The police force, recruited from Sikhs as well as Chinese, ensured motorists had right of way at street junctions, but some Chinese purposefully placed themselves in the way of motor vehicles, hoping for some injury that might gain them $25 compensation. In the last six months four had been killed this way.

Glidden and his party were guests at a 'chow chow' given to the leading bankers and merchants of Shanghai. The guests were seated eight to a table and the menu of sixty courses included such dishes as bird's nest soup, stewed bamboo shoots and shark's fin soup. After a little practise, which amused other guests, the Gliddens mastered the use of chopsticks. Hot rice wine was served in small porcelain cups. After dinner those fond of tobacco and opium had a smoke.

# 18

# IMPERIAL JAPAN

They sailed from Shanghai on 21 April 1906 aboard SS *Manchuria* bound for Yokohama. Shortly before sailing, the trans-Pacific cable brought news of the San Francisco earthquake which caused great concern for all Americans on board, particularly the ship's captain whose family lived in the devastated city. On arrival in Japan they heard that first reports had, if anything, understated the scale of the disaster.

After crossing the Yellow Sea the *Manchuria* called at Nagasaki, where the dockyards were hard at work building several large naval vessels as well as repairing others captured from Russia.

As soon as the anchor was dropped coal lighters came alongside. Men filled 20-pound baskets of coal, which women and children carried to the ship's bunkers. Eight hundred labourers took twelve hours to load 3,000 tons of coal.

The following day they sailed across the inland sea to Kobe where they met with a series of curious, not to say suspicious, difficulties. Three months earlier Glidden had sent a cable requesting an English-speaking guide who could act as an interpreter. The guide who presented himself was not who they expected. They were told the original guide had accepted another position, but failed to let anyone know, so a substitute had been found.

Another twenty-four hours brought them to Yokohama. The Napier cleared customs without difficulty and Glidden was able to present a letter from the New York office of the Standard Oil Company, asking their Japanese agents to supply petrol which was to be delivered to depots along his intended route.

The road to Tokyo took them through villages of low, thatched houses belonging to fishermen, rice farmers and vegetable growers. Japanese horses did not take well to the Napier. The owner of one startled animal threw a stone at the car, making a large dent.

They found Tokyo crowded with people, all there to celebrate Japan's victory over Russia. Captured guns were on display in the grounds of the Imperial Palace. Army officers were telling groups of visiting children how each of the massive guns was captured. It was all part of an effort to prepare boys to become the

A captured Russian gun in the grounds of the Imperial Palace, Japan. (Author's collection)

soldiers of future wars. Every house flew the national flag and everything was being done to encourage a spirit of patriotism.

Glidden, through his contacts at the US legation, succeeded in acquiring admission tickets for a grand military parade at which the Emperor and Empress were to be present. The occasion was formal, requiring Glidden and Charles Thomas to wear frock coats and silk top hats while Mrs Glidden wore her best morning gown. They were given a place on a viewing platform reserved for distinguished guests, where they stood for three hours before the ceremony began. Japan's victorious generals and admirals received enthusiastic applause as they took their positions. Finally the Emperor appeared, riding in a superb carriage, followed by a second carriage containing the Crown Prince. They passed in front of the troops before the Emperor seated himself on a throne, ready for the march past that concluded the ceremony.

Twenty miles south of Yokohama was the shrine of Kamakura, where they visited several temples and saw a large statue of the Buddha. Returning along a narrow road, a local farmer, forced to make way, took out his anger by throwing three large stones at the car. Luckily all of them missed. Further on the Napier sank to its wheel hubs in mud. A grinning crowd gathered to watch but were completely unwilling to help, a marked contrast with the attitude of people in other countries.

Preparations were made for a drive south to Kobe over the Tōkaidō, the East Sea Road, the most important of the five imperial roads established in the Edo Period. The Napier would be the first car to travel this historic route, which ran along the coast of Honshu Island. They meant to leave on 4 May but, again, there was a problem finding a guide and interpreter. One candidate for the job excused himself saying, 'I sorry, I afraid motorcar; too much dust, too fast, kill people, cannot go with you.' Apparently all the professional tourist guides had decided that motoring was not for them. They preferred parties they could take into Tokyo's shops where they received commission. A number of them even refused $2 in gold. Finally one active and intelligent man presented himself. Glidden's first question was, 'Have you been in Manchuria?'

'Yes,' was the reply, 'and I have slept on the snow.'

He claimed to have served as a spy in the war with Russia and proved to be a very capable guide, though he always behaved in a very superior manner. Hotel staff all greeted him with three deep ceremonial bows, which he acknowledged with a single bow. That done, he would light a cigarette and leave Glidden and Charles Thomas to unload the luggage without him. Later he would take a bath in his own room, then change his European dress for traditional costume. The deference he received from other Japanese, together with the circumstances

Glidden's Japanese interpreter, who may also have been a police spy. (Author's collection / *Boston Sunday Globe*)

surrounding his employment, led them to suspect that he was an agent of the Japanese security service, there to keep an eye on them.

During their drive to Kobe, they passed innumerable small farms worked entirely by hand. In America they would have been regarded as mere gardens. Everywhere preparations were being made to welcome soldiers home from the war. At the entrance of each village stood a triumphal arch made of bamboo and the national flag and decorative lanterns hung from all the houses. In one village, officers were drilling 7-year-old children. In another, they saw ranks of uniformed boys marching along the street carrying wooden rifles. At intervals the Napier stopped at neat, attractive tea houses where service was provided by girls wearing elegant kimonos.

A rough, badly engineered road over steep cliffs took them round Sagami Bay to Atami, a popular resort on the Dzu peninsular 70 miles from Tokyo, where they stayed in a clean, comfortable inn.

Before the Napier lay a difficult climb to the head of the Hakone Pass, which no motor vehicle had yet crossed. The road was very bad and a lot of hard work and trouble would have been saved had they hired a team of horses to pull the

**Japan**
April – May 1906

1 Nagasaki
2 Tokyo
3 Atami
4 Hakone
5 Hamamatsu
6 Nagoya
7 Kyoto
8 Kobe
9 Osaka
10 Nikko

Japan's militarism. Uniformed boys parade along a village street. (Author's collection / *The Autocar*)

car over. The distance was no more than 6 miles but it took them eight hours, negotiating severe hairpin bends every hundred feet and gradients as steep as 20 per cent. In some places the road was under repair, but here at least the workmen were willing to haul the car along on the end of a rope.

At the summit they were rewarded with the finest view in all Japan. To their left was the Pacific Ocean, dotted with islands; in the foreground a vast plain with scattered villages and, towering above all else, Mount Fuji.

Descending from the pass, they drove for 25 miles through villages set so close to each other that it was impossible to see where their boundaries were. There were no traffic regulations. In one place they asked a policeman what the rule of the road was. He replied, 'There is no rule. Get along the best you can. You have a big rickshaw; drive in the centre and go slow.'

Unused to motor vehicles, no one paid attention to the sound of the horn and on occasion frightened horses became uncontrollable and had to be unhitched from their carts. Most trying of all were the hordes of children playing in the street; young girls carrying baby brothers or sisters on their backs and small boys

Climbing the Hakone Pass. One of the few times Glidden photographed Charles Thomas at the Napier's wheel. (Author's collection)

who would run out from a side street and plunge between the Napier's wheels. Great care was needed to avoid a serious accident.

That evening they arrived at an inn where naked men and women were bathing together in large tubs of hot water without any concern for modesty or the presence of foreigners. The inn was built at the far end of a bamboo bridge of twenty-five spans which crossed the Fuji River. Unconvinced of its strength, Glidden had thirty men stand on one of the spans before he would venture across in the Napier. Even then he had all baggage and heavy supplies unloaded first. The Napier's weight caused each span to sink by 2ft, which meant the use of high revs and a low gear to climb over to the next section.

Because of all the lost time caused by crossing the small bridge, they were forced to stop for the night at Gwabuchi, 20 miles short of their intended destination. They took rooms at a rural inn, but the Napier had to be left out in the open where it attracted a large crowd. Their guide exerted his authority and arranged for a bamboo fence to be erected round the car, after which the crowd disappeared.

The inn was run in the traditional Japanese way. To preserve the highly polished floors no shoes were worn indoors and the stairs were as steep as a ladder. Their rooms were empty, save for matting on the floor, but a girl appeared with cushions and a table all of 8 inches high, upon which they were served tea. Supper consisted of chicken and fish, both fried in what Glidden described as the same tasteless batter. At ten o'clock quilts were spread on the floor and they were given huge padded dressing gowns to cover themselves. These proved too hot when on, but they found themselves too cold if they took them off. They got little sleep and in the morning found themselves covered in flea bites.

The following day they set out to find a bridge over the next river, which involved a detour on narrow roads among paddy fields. They were moving at 15mph when the road gave way and they came to a sudden halt, half overturned in a ditch. Luckily no one was hurt and a timber wagon, following behind, provided planks which aided them in getting the car back on the road.

After recovering from this mishap, the day's run took them past interesting scenes of village life. They saw craftsmen at work carving, papermaking, weaving and decorating pottery. In the tea gardens women and children were harvesting leaves for semi-naked men to process.

At Hamamatsu, halfway between Tokyo and Kobe, they put up for the night at one of Japan's best inns. A crowd of people gathered around the car, loosening nuts and altering leavers, not with any malicious intent but simply curious about this strange new machine.

They were well treated in the Hamamatsu inn but it provided Mr Glidden with one of his more startling experiences. Seeking the bathroom, he discovered it being happily shared by two men and four women, all bathing together. Considering the room too crowded, he quietly withdrew.

A long day's drive over a mountain on a well graded road brought them to Nagoya where the hotel proprietor was unhelpful and the police kept close watch on them, stopping them several times, taking their names and asking their destination.

Leaving Nagoya on the morning of 9 May, long detours were needed to find suitable ferries across two rivers. In both cases it was necessary to lash boats together and build a platform to hold the car. At five that afternoon they crossed a chain of mountains on a steep zigzag road which forced them to climb one section forwards and the next in reverse. The day's drive lasted twelve hours and they did not reach Kyoto until after dark.

On 11 May they drove south to Nara with mountains on either hand. On the way they met two pilgrims, a married couple, who were walking to all the Buddhist temples in Japan. Before starting they had gone to their local temple and given away all their possessions, save for the clothes on their backs. Aided by a

One of the Buddhist pilgrims met on the road to Nara. (Author's collection)

The Japanese guide oversees as Charles Thomas positions the Napier for a precarious ferry crossing. (Author's collection / *Boston Sunday Globe*)

small handbell, they begged for food in every village along their 1,000-mile route. They agreed to be photographed and, in return for a small gift, gave the Napier their blessing.

Situated in hill country, Nara possessed many Shinto gates and one of Japan's principal Shinto temples where girls danced to music played by three priests. Around the temple stood numerous stone lanterns donated by persons hoping for good fortune and a long and happy life. The lanterns were lit every night, provided their donor had paid the yearly fee.

The ferry across the River Tonegawa on the way to Nikko. (Author's collection)

They found Osaka to be a city of elaborately carved and decorated temples. One street was lined with temples for nearly a mile and led to the great Tennoji temple which housed what was claimed to be the largest bell in the world.

From Osaka the last 45 miles to Kobe were completed in pouring rain. The road was bad, full of holes, and a bridge was down which forced a long detour. They came across a procession of wailing men winding their way along a village street, followed by a decorated bullock cart loaded with provisions. These were being taken to the temple where they would be placed before the image of Buddha in memory of friends and relatives killed in the war with Russia. After the ceremony the priests would take some of the food for themselves and give what remained to the poor.

Nothing would persuade Glidden to drive back to Tokyo over the inferior roads by which they had reached Kobe, and so the car was returned to the capital by train. Now the plan was to go north to see the shrines and mausoleums of the Tokugawa Shoguns at Nikko.

Before leaving Tokyo, Japanese friends invited them to a traditional dinner at the famous Maple club. The occasion took place in a private room with matting on the floor. They sat at low tables and fifteen courses were served and eaten with chopsticks. Many of the dishes were fish, both raw and cooked. Between courses there was music while girls in traditional costume danced.

The road north from Tokyo, the Oshu Kaido, was said to be in excellent condition but it proved to be difficult. There was no bridge at the River Tonegawa, which forced them to use a small, precarious ferry on which all four of the Napier's wheels overhung the sides.

They found Nikko to be very picturesque, with snow-capped mountains and valleys full of flowering azaleas. Streams wound through ravines with cascades spanned by footbridges painted red and green. Unfortunately the magnificent temples and mausoleums were being repaired and were covered in scaffolding.

On 29 May Mr and Mrs Glidden sailed from Yokohama aboard the Pacific Mail steamer *Siberia*, bound for San Francisco. Glidden was anxious to see what the earthquake had done to the city. The car was shipped directly to Boston by way of Seattle and the Northern Pacific railroad.

During his time in Japan Charles Thomas had developed a grumbling appendix. He received treatment in a Japanese hospital but did not have it removed. Instead Japanese doctors used ice packs to reduce the pain and inflammation. He saw the car safely to Boston and then continued home to England where he did have an operation. He spent the summer recuperating in the company of the bride he had not seen since shortly after their honeymoon the previous October. By the autumn of 1906 Glidden was ready to be off again and Charles was recalled to Boston.

# 19

# DOWN MEXICO WAY

This time the journey was to be south, across the United States into Mexico and, again, a substantial part of it was to be made on railroad tracks. They left Boston on 1 November with a cold northerly wind blowing. For the first time Mrs Glidden had a female travelling companion, a Miss Waldron. The journey had been brought to the attention of the White House and Glidden was to carry a letter of greeting from President Theodore Roosevelt to President Porfirio Diaz of Mexico.

They first drove to Washington to collect the letter and then turned north and went by way of the battlefield at Gettysburg to Syracuse in upper New York State. Glidden had driven to Chicago once already and had no wish to repeat the experience, so the car was then sent there by train and the railroad wheels fitted.

On 22 November the Napier left Chicago bound for Kansas City and then El Paso on the US–Mexico border. From Kansas City they became the second section of a scheduled train running ahead of a fast mail express. They kept ahead for 50 miles, but the weather was bad and they had to be side tracked.

It was an unusually cold winter and on 1 December they were snowbound at Santa Rosa, New Mexico. However, on reaching El Paso they did not cross the border but, still on the railroad, turned east across Texas to Little Rock in Arkansas. From there they took the tracks of the Frisco and Cotton Belt Railroad to Fort Worth, Dallas, Houston, Galveston, San Antonio and Laredo, where they finally crossed into Mexico.

As on the Canadian Pacific they carried a conductor and their movements were controlled by the railroad dispatchers. Glidden ensured publicity by carrying newspaper reporters from the various cities through which they passed.

Their luck runs out. (*The Autocar*)

On 31 December, 50 miles north of Mexico City, the Napier hit a stone wedged between the main and guard rails, causing it to jump the track. It ran 90ft on the sleepers and came to rest, partly overturned, against an embankment. Glidden and his companions were thrown out, shaken but not injured. More harm was done to the car; its front wheels were destroyed and both axles sprung.

Now Glidden's expertise as a telegrapher came into play. He immediately used the portable apparatus he carried to tap the track side wires and contact the local train dispatcher. The party was rescued and arrived safely in Mexico City at six o'clock the same evening. A wrecking train was sent out early the following morning to bring in the car, which was then shipped to London and put back in condition to continue the world tour.

# 20

# PARTING OF THE WAYS

The following year, 1907, Glidden retrieved the completely refurbished Napier and spent the months of August and September touring Britain. From London his route took him through Oxford and Stratford-upon-Avon, then north into Scotland where he visited Gretna Green, Edinburgh, Aberdeen and John O'Groats. After that he returned south to the Lake District, the Welsh Borders, the Wye Valley and Land's End.

His usual letter, published in the *Boston Globe*, contains bland descriptions of places visited and lists of distances travelled. Unlike previous letters, he has nothing to say, neither approval nor criticism, about the people he meets or their way of life, though he makes a point of mentioning that he was granted special permission to drive through the grounds of Balmoral, Queen Alexandra having quit the place the previous day.

The most noteworthy events of the British tour took place shortly before Glidden returned to the USA. He was given the opportunity to drive one of Napier's racing machines 75 miles round the Brooklands Circuit and, on Tuesday 10 September, he attended a luncheon at the Café Royal given in his honour by Selwyn Edge. Other guests included Montague Napier and representatives of the motoring press. Edge gave a speech in which he emphasised that Glidden's tour of the world was made in a car using its own power. He then proposed a toast to his client's health.

In reply Glidden summarised his journeys, in the course of which he had taken 2,000 photographs and written no less than 200,000 words for the *Boston Globe*. His relatively trouble-free motoring was due to the outstanding design of the car, to the care it was given by an excellent engineer and to the fact that he did not force the car beyond reasonable limits of either speed or distance travelled each day. During his world tour he had met all sorts and conditions of men from crowned heads downwards and had everywhere been met with the greatest possible enthusiasm. To the many friends he had made along the way it was his habit to send a card with details of total miles travelled. He concluded by suggesting a toast to the health of his car's talented designer. All present approved

# TOURING THE WORLD IN A MOTOR CAR.

*Yokohama, Japan, May 29th, 1906.*

| Countries. | Miles. |
|---|---|
| 1. Afridi | 41 |
| 2. Annam......crossed frontier | |
| 3. Australia* | 2,109 |
| 4. Austria | 627 |
| 5. Bajour ......crossed frontier | |
| 6. Bavaria | 295 |
| 7. Belgium | 160 |
| 8. Bohemia | 315 |
| 9. Burmah | 509 |
| 10. Canada | 1,251 |
| 11. Ceylon | 1,334 |
| 12. China | 308 |
| 13. Cochin China | 652 |
| 14. Denmark | 306 |
| 15. England | 2,639 |
| 16. Fiji | 200 |
| 17. France | 4,565 |
| 18. Germany | 1,546 |
| 19. Hawaii | 30 |
| 20. Holland | 435 |
| 21. Hongkong | 170 |
| 22. Ireland | 1,510 |
| 23. India | 4,345 |
| 24. Italy | 508 |
| 25. Japan | 1,122 |
| 26. Java | 1,250 |
| 27. New Zealand | 1,145 |
| 28. Scotland | 200 |
| 29. Spain | 30 |
| 30. Straits Settlements | 303 |
| 31. Swat | 19 |
| | 27,924 |

| Countries. | Miles. |
|---|---|
| Up. | 27,924 |
| 32. Sweden | 1,540 |
| 33. Switzerland | 1,097 |
| 34. United States | 2,612 |
| 35. Wales | 427 |
| TOTAL | 33,600 |

Car—NAPIER, LONDON.
Tyres—DUNLOP "

To make the drive of 33,600 miles in 35 Countries, I have motored 271 days twice circling the Globe; crossing the Arctic Circle in Sweden, reaching the most southerly road in the world in New Zealand and driving upon railway tracks from Minneapolis to Vancouver.

Travelling by sea 44,760 miles in 149 days.

A total journey by Motor car and steamships of 78,360 miles in 420 days.

\* Includes Tasmania.

## CHARLES J. GLIDDEN,

### Address: The Touraine. Boston. Mass.

### UNITED STATES OF AMERICA.

A copy of Glidden's mileage chart signed by Charles Thomas. (Author's collection)

the idea and the toast was drunk. Montague Napier's reply, though genuine, was brief.

Some unremarkable photographs of Glidden's tour of Britain appeared in the *Boston Globe* but there are none in Charles Thomas's albums. Being on home soil, he may not have felt the need for any, but their lack may be symptomatic of a growing strain between the Napier's owner and its engineer.

Touring with Glidden meant prolonged absences from home which, with a new wife, became increasingly difficult. Also Charles's father, Frederick, was getting on. In 1896, when the young Charles gained his original apprenticeship with Napier, Frederick Thomas started a garage business at the rear of his hotel in Rottingdean, Sussex. He intended that his younger son should, in time, take over that business. He also needed assistance in establishing a motor bus service between the hotel and the nearby town of Brighton.

Glidden had always treated his engineer with the greatest consideration and relied upon him to maintain the Napier. The many thousands of miles of trouble-free motoring in demanding conditions were undoubtedly due to Charles Thomas's technical skill. However, at all times Glidden expected deference and was not prepared to admit of any human circumstance that conflicted with his wishes. After their tour of Britain they parted company and never met again. In 1908 Glidden, with a new Napier engineer, went on to complete his world tour with a journey through Egypt, Palestine and Greece.

Charles Thomas settled in Rottingdean and inherited his father's business. During the First World War he joined the Air Inspection Department based at Waddon, on what was to become Croydon Aerodrome, where he helped certify aircraft as mechanically sound for front-line service. He would ride into Brighton on a motorcycle and then take a train from the station to work. After the war he maintained his interest in aviation. Napier-powered seaplanes won two of the famous Schneider Trophy races and he travelled to watch them whenever they were flown over the Solent. He had four children, a daughter and three sons. Always a heavy smoker he died of cancer in 1941.

After 1908 Glidden became interested in aeronautics, became qualified as a balloon pilot and made many ascents over New England, during one of which he was shot at by a farmer.

On America's entry into the First World War he served as a first lieutenant, and later as captain, in the Aviation Division of the Signal Corps. His post was that of president of the aviation examining board, charged with selecting recruits who wished to become aviators and signallers. After his discharge from regular service he became a major in the Reserve Corps, later being promoted to lieutenant colonel. Thereafter he was known to many as 'Colonel Glidden'. He and his wife had no children and he died of cancer in 1927.

# Index

If you enjoyed this book, you may also be interested in…

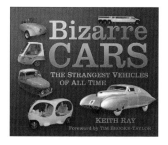

## Bizarre Cars
KEITH RAY

This book is dedicated to a select group of designers and marketing people round the world who, in blissful ignorance of the meaning of 'fit for purpose', came up with vehicles so totally bizarre, ugly or inappropriate (in some cases all three) that they must be recorded for posterity. From the Tata/MDI OneCAT, which runs entirely on air and has a range of 7km, to the Russian ZIS 101 Sport, based on a limousine and the longest two-seater sports car of all time, the cars herein will raise a smile and few eyebrows!

978 0 7524 8771 7

## 100 Years of the British Automobile Racing Club
GARETH ROGERS

From a group of enthusiasts who took their fragile hybrid machines on a run through the Surrey countryside in December 1912, to the club's present involvement in Grand Prix racing in India, this wonderful book is a must have for all fans of motorsport. The history of the BARC is as much a history of British motor-racing, from the old cyclecars to the modern Forumla One, as it is of the prestigious club itself. With rare illustrations, here is the ultimate history of one of the most important institutions in motorsport.

978 0 7524 6180 9

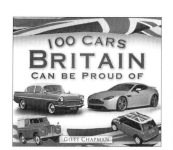

## 100 Cars Britain Can Be Proud Of
GILES CHAPMAN

From Ace to Zodiac – via the world-beating Land Rover, the thrilling Morgan Aeromax, the eternally young Mini Cooper and the unique London taxi – this is a celebration of the best British cars, old and new, in all their glorious diversity. Inside, you'll find out about the country's 100 most significant models, boasting style, speed, ingenuity and The Right Stuff. They'll make you glad they're British!

978 0 7524 5686 7

## Blood, Sweat and Tyres
DAVID LONG

With a quarter of million cars a day crowding onto the M25, and millions more standing nose-to-tail on our A-roads, Britain is now officially Europe's largest car park. *Blood, Sweat and Tyres* casts a wry eye over the world of modern motoring, highlighting some of its strangest bizarre aspects. Find out why the most successful Le Mans driver of all time wishes he could race a 90-year-old lady; how it is we know Shakespeare wasn't a petrolhead; why the Fab Three bullied Ringo into selling his favourite French supercar, and much more.

978 0 7524 5488 7

Visit our website and discover thousands of other History Press books.

## www.thehistorypress.co.uk

The History Press